**Cambridge English R**

**Level 6**

Series editor: Philip Prowse

# *Trumpet Voluntary*

## Jeremy Harmer

**CAMBRIDGE**
UNIVERSITY PRESS

# CAMBRIDGE
## UNIVERSITY PRESS

University Printing House, Cambridge CB2 8BS, United Kingdom

Cambridge University Press is part of the University of Cambridge.

It furthers the University's mission by disseminating knowledge in the pursuit of education, learning and research at the highest international levels of excellence.

www.cambridge.org
Information on this title: www.cambridge.org/9780521666190

First published 1999
Reprinted 2015

Printed in the United Kingdom by Hobbs the Printers Ltd

*A catalogue record for this publication is available from the British Library*

ISBN 978-0-521-66619-0 Paperback

# Contents

# Characters

*Protagonist (主役)*

**Derek Armstrong:** a viola player.

**Malgosia Armstrong:** a trumpet player. Derek's wife.

**Tibor Arkadi:** a pianist and trumpet player.

**Rosemary Green:** an editor. A friend of Malgosia's.

**Carl Robins:** a violinist.

**Rachel Merino:** a cellist.

**Matt Jenkins:** a violinist.

**Ken Awolowo:** a law student from Nigeria.

**Teresa Kowalewska:** Malgosia's mother.

**Jacek Kowalewski:** Malgosia's father.

**Anja Kowalewska:** Malgosia's sister.

**Sandra Andrade:** a Brazilian student in Rio de Janeiro.

**Oswaldo Morales:** a Cuban private detective.

**Paul Brewster:** an English teacher in Rio de Janeiro.

**Two policemen.**

**Rachel's mother.**

喇叭

**trumpet** – *noun*. a musical instrument which the player blows into. It has three valves which the player uses to change the notes.

隨意的

**voluntary** – *adj*. describes something you do willingly without being made to do it, and without being given money for it.

'Trumpet Voluntary' – the name of a piece of music for trumpet by the composer Jeremiah Clarke (1659–1707) who killed himself after being disappointed in love.

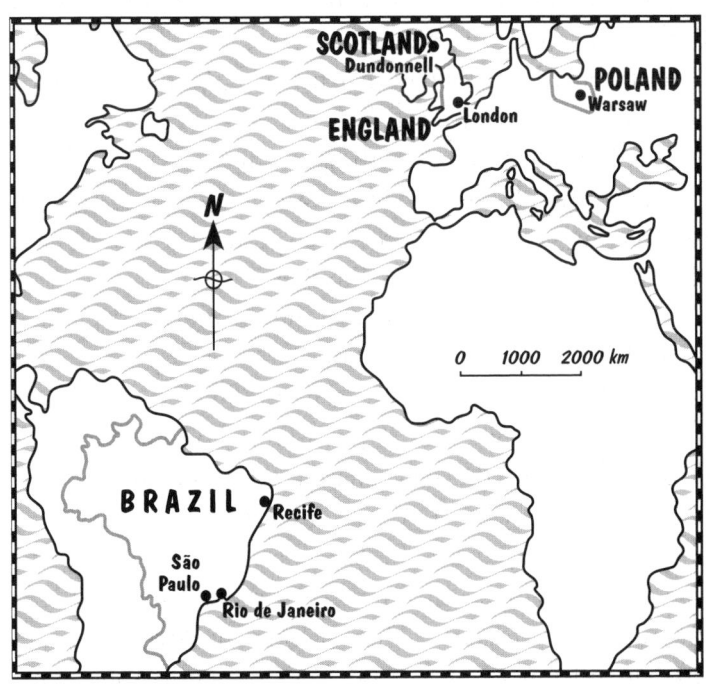

# Chapter 1 *The silent house*

It seems impossible to feel so happy and so sad all at the same time. Laughter and tears. Not what you would expect for someone in my situation. Maybe, in time, the future, in which I am so confident, will cancel out the bad memories of the past. There's so much to look forward to, after all. But there's so much to remember too.

It all started on the day that my wife disappeared. Well no, that's not quite true. It had started a long time before that, only I didn't know anything about it. That just shows you how stupid I was. Things were happening right in front of my nose, and I never even realised. I should have seen the signs, but I was blind to them.

On that particular day, I came home after a rehearsal. I opened the door and walked into the house. I put my viola case on the floor, took off my coat, and hung it up. Then I took my viola into our music room. I wanted to look through some of the new quartet music before the next rehearsal. That's when I noticed my wife's old trumpet, the one she had played for the last ten years. It wasn't in its case. It was on top of the piano, as if she'd abandoned it in the middle of a practice. That was strange. My wife always left her instrument in its case. Perhaps she had just gone upstairs for a minute. But then I noticed the silence in the house. You could feel it.

I went into the kitchen. There was a coffee cup in the sink. It hadn't been washed. That was strange too. My wife never left dirty cups in the sink. I went upstairs. The bed was unmade. Now I was really worried. Then I noticed the cupboard. It was open, emptier than usual. Suddenly I started to get frightened. I ran into the middle bedroom, the room she used as an office. I opened the cupboard door there. One of our suitcases was missing.

For a moment I stood there, my mind refusing to accept what was in front of my eyes. I thought somebody had taken her clothes and stolen her suitcase. Then I remembered the trumpet on the piano. Perhaps she had gone somewhere? But where? Why hadn't she told me? Then I thought, oh no, perhaps someone has kidnapped her, forced her to go away. But something told me this wasn't true, and I sat down on the chair in front of her computer. I tried to think but all I could see was her face, last night, in that Italian restaurant, smiling at me through the candle flame. She had been so kind, so beautiful. We hadn't argued at all. It was the happiest evening for ages. I thought everything was all right again.

I looked out of the window at the park behind our house. Half past five in the afternoon on a beautiful late August afternoon. Children were playing in the sunshine. The old man was walking his dog, talking to it sometimes, before pulling it forward on its lead. He walked his dog at the same time every day. Malgosia and I used to watch him and laugh together, but lately we hadn't been laughing very much at all.

And that's when I knew, suddenly, that she had gone for good. That's why she was so loving yesterday. She was saying goodbye.

I rushed downstairs to the hall, my heart beating far too

fast. I couldn't find our address book in its usual place. I ran into the music room and got my electronic organiser from my viola case. My fingers were shaking so much that it was difficult to make the damn thing work but I found Rosemary's number in the end and dialled it. Rosemary was my wife's best friend.

'Rosemary,' I said when she answered, 'where is Malgosia? Where's she gone?'

'Who is this?' she answered, confused. 'Derek, is that you?'

'Yes,' I said, 'of course it's me. Where is she?'

'Derek, what's the matter? You sound terrible. What are you talking about?'

'Malgosia,' I said, 'where is she?'

'I don't know,' Rosemary said. I could hear her children in the background. 'Isn't she there?'

'Of course she isn't here. That's why I'm asking you,' I shouted.

'There's no need to talk to me like that,' she said angrily. I forced myself to calm down and apologised. Rosemary asked me to tell her what the matter was. So I did.

'You're not going to like this, Derek,' she said when I had finished, 'but I haven't got any idea where she is. I mean, I knew you weren't that happy together –'

'What?' I interrupted. 'What did you say?'

She must have been worried by the tone of my voice.

'Oh nothing,' she said, 'nothing. Just that Margie' – that's what she called her – 'said that sometimes you and she . . . well, that life wasn't always very much fun.'

'So you knew she was going to leave?' I insisted.

'No. No, of course I didn't,' Rosemary replied, and I wondered whether to believe her. 'Look, Derek,' she went on, 'I'm sorry. I've got to go. But I'll ring you this evening, all right. I don't know anything about this, honestly.'

'You can't go now,' I cried. I was desperate.

'Hey, Derek,' she said, cutting in. 'It's Wednesday, isn't it?'

'Yes, but –'

'So have you rung the theatre? They might know something.'

The theatre. Of course. Why hadn't I thought of that? I slammed down the telephone receiver without saying goodbye. Then I picked it up again and dialled the number of the Drury Lane Theatre Royal. That's where Malgosia was playing trumpet three nights a week in the musical 'Miss Saigon'.

In a few minutes I was talking to Duncan Gardner, the musical director of the orchestra for the show.

'Duncan,' I said, 'is Malgosia there?'

'No. Of course not.'

'Why "of course not"?' I asked.

'She's left the band,' he said, sounding surprised.

'She's what?'

'Derek,' he said, 'what's going on? I don't understand. She said that she was going away. I thought she was going somewhere with you.'

'Do you know where she was going?' I asked.

'Derek, what on earth is going on?'

'Did she say where she was going?' I asked again.

'No. She just said she was leaving England.'

'Leaving England?!'

9

'Yes,' he said, 'leaving England.'

I sat there with my mind in chaos. Leaving England? But where was she going? The world is a big place.

'Derek, Derek, are you all right?' I heard Duncan say.

'Sure,' I replied, 'I'm fine,' and I put down the receiver. I looked at myself in the mirror above the telephone and saw my terrified face, the face of a man whose wife had left him. I felt like a fool.

I didn't want to make the next call, but I couldn't think what else to do. I dialled the number of Malgosia's parents in Warsaw. Perhaps my wife had run back to Poland, her country, the country she had left when she came to study music in London ten years before.

Someone picked up the phone in Warsaw. They spoke in Polish, which was not surprising, of course, but it is a language I have never been able to use.

'Hello,' I said, 'is that Teresa?' Teresa is Malgosia's mother. The voice on the other end said something more in Polish. I couldn't understand a word of it.

'Can I speak to Teresa?' I said, 'This is Derek. From England. Malgosia's husband.'

There was a silence at the other end of the line. Then the voice started speaking again, quickly, trying to tell me something. I suddenly realised that it was Malgosia's grandmother. She didn't speak a word of English and I couldn't say anything in Polish. So I said goodbye and put down the phone.

I went to the kitchen and got a bottle of wine. I opened it and poured myself a glass and drank it. Then I poured another. And another. I wondered what to do. It was beginning to get dark outside. I thought of Malgosia sitting at the kitchen table opposite me, the two of us sitting in silence. There had been a lot of silence recently.

I thought of Malgosia practising in the music room, the beautiful sound of her trumpet echoing through the house. Would I ever hear that sound again?

I thought of Malgosia sitting in her office, tapping at the keys of her computer, investigating all those sites on the Internet, talking to people all over the world while I stayed downstairs watching television.

Suddenly I sat up straight. That's it, I told myself, that's it. The computer. Maybe I would learn something from the computer.

I ran up to her office and switched her machine on. I went straight to her e-mails, hoping to find some clue, some indication of where she might have gone, and I was instantly rewarded.

There was a message in the file marked 'incoming mail' which she must have read earlier in the day. I pointed the mouse at it and clicked. When the message appeared I read it and then read it again, trying to understand it. The words in front of me just didn't seem to make much sense.

*Malgosia, where are you? I'll try and ring you, but in case I can't get through … Things are getting a bit difficult. Get here quick, otherwise I'll be in trouble.*
*You'll love Rio. I promise.*
*Tibor.*

\*   \*   \*

Tibor! It was the first time I had heard that name for many years. Of course it might not be the Tibor I was thinking of, but somehow, in my heart, I knew immediately that it was and I felt all the anger and hurt all over again.

There was a loud knocking at the front door. I switched off the computer and went downstairs. So much had happened that I couldn't think straight. Tibor? Rio? Did that mean Rio de Janeiro? I opened the door.

Two policemen were standing there.

'Mr Armstrong?' one of them said.

'Yes,' I answered. 'What's happened? Is something wrong?' The police only come to your door when something terrible has happened.

'Is Mrs Armstrong in?' the first policeman asked, ignoring my question. 'Malgosia Armstrong,' he said, pronouncing it with an 's' sound instead of the 'sh' sound it should have.

'No, no she isn't. Why do you want her?'

'Are you sure she isn't here, sir?' the second policeman said.

'Of course I'm sure,' I answered back. 'Why? What's this all about?'

'We just want to ask Mrs Armstrong a few questions,' said the first policeman.

'Questions? What about?' I asked.

'I think, sir,' said the first policeman, 'it would be a good idea if we came inside, don't you?'

# Chapter 2   *Tibor and Malgosia*

The first time I saw my wife she was laughing. It was in the canteen at the Royal Academy of Music in Marylebone Road, London. I had arrived there two weeks before to start my three year course as a music student, studying the viola as my first instrument.

My parents hadn't wanted me to be a music student. Even my mother, for whom music was almost as important as eating and breathing, and who wanted me to love music too, thought that it wasn't the right kind of career for me if I wanted to get on in the world. Instead, she and my father wanted me to be a doctor like he was, but I was never very good at science and anyway, I hated the sight of blood. I was probably a bit of a coward I suppose. I wasn't very good at sport either.

I suppose you could say that I was always crazy about music. My mother was a fantastic pianist when I was a child. She didn't earn money from it (except for the few pupils who used to come to her for lessons at the weekend). But all through my childhood I would hear her playing beautiful music, sometimes late on summer evenings, as I lay listening in my bed. I learned to love the sound of her playing as I went to sleep. Later I realised that music, for my mother, was a secret world that she felt safe in, a world where my father was on the outside looking in, a world where she was the boss and where her imagination was set free.

13

I think my mother wanted me to discover that world too, so I started violin lessons when I was only six. I loved it immediately, and some of my happiest memories of childhood are of the times when I made music on my little violin and my mother accompanied me on the piano. Later, my teacher told me that I could change to the viola because then I would get into all the orchestras I wanted to. There are never enough viola players, he told me, so you'll always be wanted. And he was right. The moment I started on the viola I got into school orchestras and later youth orchestras with very little trouble.

Although violas are only slightly bigger than violins, you have to play them differently. They have their own unique sound. They're not superstars, like violins, but they make all the nice noises inside the music, all the beautiful harmonies. Violas are modest, but they're charming, warm, and loving, everything I hoped I could be.

Gradually, as I went through school, I spent more and more time doing music, and less and less time studying anything else. In the end my parents had to admit that I would never get to university with my poor marks, but a career in music was just a possibility. And so, even though my father really disapproved – and he told me so about three times a week – he agreed to let me go to music college to study viola and piano. It was all I could do and it was all I wanted to do.

I have a clear memory of that morning when I met Malgosia. It was two weeks into my three year course. I came down the stairs after a viola lesson which had demonstrated to me how much I still had to learn. I wasn't having much success socially, either, and just occasionally, I

14

wondered whether my father had been right. I opened the canteen doors, still nervous about being a 'new boy', still unsure about whether I really belonged there.

I walked into the canteen and queued up to get some coffee. Behind me I could hear people talking and laughing, men's voices, women's voices. I paid for my coffee and turned round.

There was a large group of people around a table. They were all listening to someone sitting next to the wall. Although I didn't know many of the other students yet, I recognised the person who was talking. He was famous at the Academy. He was a third year student and his name, I had been told, was Tibor Arkadi. He was half English, half Albanian and one of the 'characters' at college. He was a brilliant pianist and trumpet player and he was studying conducting. Everybody said he would be the next Solti, a Karajan for the twenty-first century. They said he made magic when he stood up in front of an orchestra. They said people would do anything for him, anything at all. With him they took musical risks they would never take with any of the other conducting students. And he got the girls. One third-year viola player who had talked to me – third years don't usually talk to first years – said that everyone had to fall in love with Tibor at least once. She had, she said, but she was over it now. I wasn't convinced by that last bit.

I stood and looked at him. He was sitting back in his chair, a tall, thin, dark-haired man with bright, laughing eyes and a wide, sensual mouth. Even I could see that he was incredibly good-looking. Even I could tell that he knew it. I don't think I have ever met anyone before or since who was so sure of himself.

15

He looked up and saw me standing there, a <u>frightened</u> first year with a pile of music in one hand and a cup of coffee in the other. I thought he would <u>ignore</u> me, but instead, turning to the people he was with, he said, 'Now who have we got here? What new musical being is this?'

They all turned round and looked at me, laughing at the way he had asked the question. And that's when I saw Malgosia. She was laughing too, her beautiful head thrown back on her long neck, her mouth open to <u>reveal</u> perfect white teeth, her eyes shining with happiness. She was <u>easily</u> the most beautiful woman I had ever seen, with long <u>red hair</u> falling over her shoulders. I couldn't take my eyes off her.

'Hey, whoever you are, stop <u>staring</u> at Malgosia and tell us who you are.' Tibor had spoken again, and I had to tear my eyes away from the redhead. Even then I knew, somehow, that Tibor was <u>dangerous</u>.

'I'm Derek,' I said, 'Derek Armstrong.'

'Well, Derek Armstrong, you'd better come and join us.' It felt like an order. I looked for somewhere to sit.

'Come on, you <u>Polish</u> beauty,' he said to the redhead, 'move up so that Derek can sit on your chair too.' He was laughing at me, but I could not <u>refuse</u>. I sat down and was immediately <u>aware</u> of Malgosia's <u>intoxicating perfume</u> and Tibor's <u>irresistible charm</u>.

'So,' said the handsome student of <u>conducting</u>, 'what's your <u>instrument</u>, then? What do you study?'

'Piano,' I replied nervously, 'and viola.'

'Ah,' he smiled, 'the viola.' The people round the table laughed. You have to get used to that if you're a viola player. It's the instrument that everyone makes jokes about.

'Hey,' said a young man on my left. 'What's the difference between a viola and a trampoline?'

'Oh no, not that old one,' Tibor complained.

'I don't know it,' said Malgosia at my side. She had the most beautiful voice, crisp like April frost. 'And what is a – what do you call it, a "trampoline"?'

'It's a thing that gymnasts jump on, do cartwheels, *boing boing*,' explained the joke teller, making movements with his arms.

'Oh,' said Malgosia, 'oh, I see,' and she said a word in Polish to show that she understood. Since nobody else spoke her language it was difficult to tell if she had got it right. 'So what is the difference between a viola and a trampoline?'

'Well,' said the person on my left, 'you have to take your shoes off to jump on a trampoline.'

There was a silence while the people who did not know the joke thought about it and then they laughed. So did I, even though I had heard the joke many times before. You have to laugh to show that you don't mind people making fun of you. It's like all jokes, though. When viola players tell viola jokes I think they're funny. But when other people do it I get all angry.

'Here's one I heard yesterday,' Tibor said, and instantly everyone turned towards him. 'Perhaps you know it, Derek.' I still don't know why he paid attention to me that day. Perhaps he was bored. Perhaps he was looking for a new victim. I don't believe he ever liked me.

'I don't know,' I managed to say. 'It depends.'

'OK,' he answered. 'Let's see. Here goes. Imagine that you are lost in a forest, a terrible, dark forest and you are very <u>frightened</u>, and you want to leave the forest, but you don't know the way ...' he <u>paused</u> for <u>dramatic effect</u>.

'Yes?' asked the joke teller on my left. 'Yes? Go on.'

'Thank you, Justin,' Tibor said. 'So there you are, <u>terrified</u> and afraid and it's getting dark. And suddenly you see <u>figures</u> coming <u>towards</u> you. In the darkness you <u>realise</u> that they are a pink elephant, a good viola player and a bad viola player. And you know that one of them can tell you the way out of the forest. Who do you ask?' He looked round the group. Nobody answered.

'You don't know?' he asked. 'Well then I'll tell you. You ask the bad viola player because the other two only <u>exist</u> in your <u>imagination</u>!' And he laughed. And then everyone laughed. And for some reason I went red.

'Did you like that joke?' Malgosia asked me a couple of minutes later. Tibor had got tired of me and was talking to someone else.

'Yes,' I had to say.

'I don't think you did. Not very much,' she said.

'Well, it's OK. I've heard it before.'

'Yes,' she said, 'but why do people make all these jokes about viola players? It is not the same in Poland.'

'I don't know. Why do people make jokes about <u>Irish</u> people or Bavarians or Polish people?' I said.

'That is only in America, I think,' Malgosia said, 'but perhaps it means that we have something in common, something that is the same for both of us?' She turned to me and looked at me with those big blue eyes of hers and I knew that I was lost.

'Hey, Malgosia,' Tibor said, getting up. 'We're going over to a Greek restaurant in Charlotte Street. Do you want to come?'

'Me?' she said in surprise. 'Me?' She was obviously delighted that he had asked her. 'Yes, yes of course.' She got up, forgetting me immediately, and they all marched out of the canteen leaving me sitting there, wondering if she or Tibor would ever speak to me again and whether I wanted them to or not.

# Chapter 3 *Rachel*

Tibor and Malgosia became lovers, of course. Even when I think about that now it hurts. After all this time it still hurts. But there was nothing I could have done, even if I had known how to. She fell for him almost immediately. Perhaps it was the scene in the canteen that did it for her. Perhaps it was later in some pub or café that she looked at him and felt the joyous pain that love can be. I don't know. I only know that when I realised what the situation was I thought I would die with unhappiness. Because I was crazy about her too, absolutely obsessed with the thought of her. And though we were the best of friends, and she came to cry on my shoulder every time Tibor ignored her or cheated on her, and even though I was sure she was very fond of me, still she didn't love me like I, poor fool, loved her. Instead I had to watch her eyes light up with excitement every time Tibor walked into the room. I had to learn to grin and bear it every time she cancelled one of our visits to the cinema or a folk club because she was going to be with him. I had to accept that, compared to Tibor, I would always be second best.

One afternoon, a few weeks into that first term, I went into Duke's Hall because I could hear the sound of a trumpet. I pushed open the wood and glass doors. Malgosia was on the empty stage making the most beautiful noise I had ever heard. Another student was accompanying her on the organ. They were playing the 'Trumpet Voluntary', one of the most famous English trumpet tunes there is.

I stood and listened until she had finished. Then she saw me, and smiled.

'That was beautiful,' I told her. 'I love Purcell's music.'

'It's not Purcell,' Malgosia said. 'Everybody thinks he wrote it, but it was actually written by someone called Jeremiah Clarke. I've been reading about it. Did you know,' she went on, 'he killed himself for love. It's the kind of thing they did in those days. Isn't it romantic?'

'No,' I laughed. 'It's stupid if you ask me.'

'Ah,' she replied dreamily, 'you are just a man, an English man. But to die for love! That takes a more passionate soul than yours perhaps.'

* * *

At the end of the first year, when the summer holidays began, Malgosia went back to Poland to be with her family. Right up until the moment she left I had this dream that she would invite me to visit her there, but somehow I knew that she wouldn't. My parents, who knew nothing of my romantic depression, wanted me to go on holiday with them, but with the arrogance of youth I couldn't stand the idea. I was much happier busking on the streets of London, playing for cinema queues and shopping tourists with the new student quartet I had joined at the end of the summer term. Our first violin player, Carl Robins, was rather uneasy about playing Mozart's 'Eine Kleine Nachtmusik' ten times a day (because he'd rather be attempting Shostakovich and Bartok) and Rachel Merino, our cellist,

21

was uncomfortable with the long metal spike which allowed her to play standing up.

'Still,' as Matt Jenkins, the second violinist said, 'it's good performance practice, and we're earning quite a bit of money too. No-one's complaining about that!'

It was true. People seemed to like the way we played, and my open viola case soon filled up with small change. We earned even more when a law student who lived with me came to help us by going round our audiences with a hat, asking for donations. Ken, a Nigerian, wasn't very keen on the music we played but he was a magician with the hat. He almost ran around the crowds that were listening to us, smiling at them, laughing and joking, telling them we were poor refugees, anything to make them put their hands in their pockets. It looked like it was going to be a good summer. Sometimes I even forgot about Malgosia. But not for long.

One evening, as we packed up our instruments for the day, Rachel suggested that we go to a pub by the river in Chiswick where she lived. The next day was Sunday so we weren't going to play, and anyway we needed a break. The others didn't want to go all that way because it's a long journey from central London but I had nothing better to do, so I agreed.

It was a lovely evening. Rachel and I sat outside and watched the life of the river in front of us. There were birds, the sounds of a great city all around us, planes starting their final approach to Heathrow airport, rowers shouting orders at each other, and a little police boat making its way down river, its blue light flashing as it went as fast as it could towards some emergency.

I liked Rachel. She was quiet and gentle. She had light brown hair, and pretty, brown eyes set in a round, pleasant face. When she smiled she looked like a happy child and you knew you could trust her. She was very easy to be with.

That night we sat and talked about what we hoped for the future. I told her I wanted to make enough money as a musician to have a nice house, travel a bit, that kind of thing. She told me that her dreams were much the same. She wanted children one day, she said, but for that she'd need to find the right man.

'Well it's no good looking at me,' I said, as a joke.

'I know that, you fool,' she said, laughing at me. 'You can't see anybody anyway. Not while Malgosia is in the way.' I blushed.

'Maybe,' I replied. I didn't like talking about it.

'Can I say something?' Rachel asked, nervously.

'It depends what it is,' I replied. Around us people were talking and laughing as the night got darker. I saw the lights of a party boat travelling along the river in front of us.

'It's just that, well, I know Malgosia is beautiful. I mean really beautiful. I wish I was beautiful like that. And I do like her. But she's crazy about Tibor, and anyone who's crazy about Tibor, well ...' She stopped and looked at me, wondering how I would react.

'Well what?' I answered. I understood what she was saying, I think, but I didn't like anyone criticising Malgosia.

'Oh God, now you're cross with me,' Rachel said. 'Sorry. Sorry. But it's just a pity to see you and her. She's not right for you. You're wasting your time, wasting your life on her

23

and you're not getting anything back. It doesn't look good. That's my opinion.'

'Well,' I snapped back, without thinking, 'I don't care what your opinion is, OK? Me and Malgosia, well, we're ...' I wanted a word that meant more than 'friend' but I couldn't think of the right one, 'we're special, all right? So it's none of your business. Just keep out of my affairs, OK?'

Rachel had gone red and I had gone too far. My only excuse is that I was very confused then, and still very young. But I suppose, if I am honest, that wasn't it. It was because Rachel had said something that I didn't want to hear because it was the truth. Now I think that if only I had listened to her then, if only I had understood what she was trying to tell me, I might not have made the decisions that I did and my life might have turned out very differently.

We finished our drinks in silence. I tried to start conversations again once or twice, but she only answered with 'yes' or 'no', so it wasn't much good. In the end, when closing time was called by the pub landlord, we just said goodbye and I caught the tube back into London.

As the train made its way noisily through the darkness I thought about the conversation I had just had and I realised that it probably meant the end of the quartet.

'Oh well,' I thought, 'I can join another one, or we'll find a new cellist. It doesn't matter.'

And then I suddenly saw Rachel's face, Rachel's sad gentle face, and perhaps it was the drink, or perhaps it was because it was a warm summer's night, or perhaps I was just lonely, I don't know, but anyway, at the next station I got off the train, walked over the bridge and got on the first train which was going back the way I had just come.

Half an hour later I was at the door of Rachel's house. I rang the bell. The door opened.

'Derek,' Rachel said in surprise, 'I thought you had gone home.'

'I was going to,' I replied, 'and then I just thought ...' but I didn't really know what I had thought so I kissed her instead. She didn't seem to mind so I kissed her again, and it was very nice and soon just kissing didn't seem to be enough and, well, you can imagine the rest.

The next morning we couldn't look at each other. We had gone too far, too fast. All I could think was that I had somehow betrayed Malgosia (which was ridiculous, since she didn't love me), and all Rachel could think was, that I had used her.

It was raining when I reached the tube station. I didn't feel good and wondered how to cheer myself up. When I got back to my house the first thing Ken said to me was,

'Where have you been? You look awful.'

'Thanks,' I said, 'thanks a lot.'

'Hey, don't you worry about it. You can sleep it off, whatever it was,' Ken said.

'I don't know,' I answered.

'Well, how about a coffee while you're thinking about it?' he offered, so we sat and talked and I told him about Rachel, even though I knew I shouldn't. But I needed someone to talk to.

'Well,' he said when I had finished my story of the previous night, 'things like that don't happen to me over here. Not yet anyway. You're just lucky.'

'Then why don't I feel lucky?' I asked him.

25

'Well now,' he laughed, 'I can't help you there. Maybe you're crazy or something. Yes, that's probably it,' and we laughed, and after half an hour in his company I felt better because he didn't seem to think that I had done anything terrible, and because he let me tell him about Malgosia and he didn't say that I was wasting my time.

*　*　*

The next day the quartet met up outside Covent Garden tube station as we had done every day since we started busking. I wasn't sure whether Rachel would be there, but she had already arrived when I got out of the lift which had brought me up from the depths of London and walked out into the sunshine. She avoided my eyes and wouldn't talk to me at first, but later, when we were setting up at one end of the old market building and the other two were getting their violins out of their cases, she came up to me.

'Derek,' she said, 'can we have a quick word?'

'Yes,' I said nervously.

'It's just this,' she announced seriously, looking away from me, 'what happened happened, I know that, but it's not going to happen again, is it?'

'No,' I said, and I meant it.

'Right,' she said in a controlled way. 'And you want the quartet to continue, don't you?'

'Yes. Yes, I think so.'

'So can we just be friends?' she asked. I wonder how much that cost her.

'If that's OK,' I said. I felt a great sense of relief, to be honest. I had expected more problems than this.

'Yes, it is OK,' she said and started to walk away. But

then she turned back, came right up to me, and for the first time that day she looked me full in the eyes.

'One last thing,' she whispered. 'I don't want anyone else knowing about our … knowing about it. And we won't talk about it ever again. OK?'

'OK,' I agreed. She relaxed then, smiled at me, walked away again and before long we were halfway through the first movement of the Mozart and the money was falling into Ken's hat.

But one afternoon two weeks later when we broke for lunch, Rachel refused to go on playing, and she wouldn't say why, and that was the end of our little band. At least for the time being.

We watched her walking away, her head down. She hadn't said goodbye to anyone.

'What was that all about?' Carl asked as Rachel disappeared round a corner. 'Does anyone know what's going on?'

We all looked at each other. Nobody had any idea.

'What about you, Ken?' Matt said, as our money-collector came towards us with four pints of beer on an old bar tray from the pub behind us.

'What about what?' Ken answered.

'Why did Rachel go off like that? Do you know?'

'Me?' said Ken. 'Why should I know? Don't ask me. Must be some musician thing. Why are you asking me?'

'Hey,' I told him, 'don't be so defensive. I'm sure it wasn't your fault.' But of course it was. His fault and my fault. Rachel and Ken had been walking towards the pub together (Ken told me later), and he'd asked her how she felt about me now. And Rachel had said, 'What do you mean?' and Ken had answered, 'You know, after that night of yours, that night together?' And Rachel had stopped in the middle of the street, gone bright red, and said, 'Who told you that? How do you know that? Did Derek tell you that?' her voice getting louder with every question. Then she'd marched past Ken, packed up her cello, told us she was leaving, and walked away without a word of farewell.

*   *   *

The summer holidays ended and the autumn term at the Academy began. There was no sign of Malgosia the first day, and she hadn't answered either of the letters I had sent her, so I was pretty miserable. I tried to talk to Rachel, but she refused to speak to me. I asked her, begged her to play with us again, and all she said was, 'How can I play with you again? You told Ken all about us, didn't you? Why should I spend any more time in your company than I have to?'

Things also weren't going well with my studies. My viola teacher was ill and the man who took her place for that first week didn't like me and I felt the same about him. My piano playing wasn't getting much better either. Carl and Matt wanted to get another cellist for our quartet, but somehow I could not agree to that. I had already done enough damage there, and I still hoped, one day, that Rachel would change her mind. And Ken wouldn't talk to me because I had lost my temper with him about what he had said to Rachel.

So I suppose you could say that my life was a mess. I was playing badly. I didn't have many friends, and the person I thought I loved had disappeared from my life.

But not for long. One evening, six days after term

started, I was sitting in my room watching a bad old Hollywood movie on my small television when someone knocked at my door. I opened it. Ken stood outside.

'Hi,' I said, 'come in. You haven't been around for a few days. Where have you been?'

'Don't worry about where I've been,' he replied, not looking me in the eye. 'You've got more important things to think about.'

'What do you mean?'

'There's someone downstairs to see you,' he said, 'and she doesn't look very happy.'

'Who is it?' I asked him.

'I don't know,' he replied. 'I've never seen her before, but she's really lovely. If you're not interested, just let me know. I'd love to try and cheer her up.'

I left him and walked downstairs. The front door was still open. It was beginning to get dark outside and a heavy rain was falling. Malgosia was standing in the passageway with two suitcases, her beautiful hair dripping wet and a look of complete misery on her face.

# Chapter 4   *The new trumpet*

'I was really excited when Tibor came to Warsaw,' Malgosia told me as I put on the kettle to make her a coffee. 'I went to meet him at the airport, I had told my family all about him. They were a bit suspicious because he was the first man I had talked about like that, but they were interested to meet him.'

I gave Malgosia a cup of coffee. She had dried her hair and changed into some fresh clothes. She looked thinner and whiter than I remembered.

'So what was the problem?' I asked. 'You met him at the airport. It must have been fantastic.' Malgosia was so involved in her own thoughts that I don't think she heard the note of bitterness in my voice.

'Oh, it was fine at first,' she replied. 'He was so pleased to see me, and I, well I was ecstatic. He came out of those sliding doors with a big grin on his face and we threw our arms around each other and I ...'

'It sounds great,' I said. I really didn't want to hear the details of this happy romance after all.

'Well, it was. I drove him back to my parents' house, and everything was absolutely fine. Even my grandparents got on with him, although he doesn't speak any Polish. But he speaks a bit of Russian, so they managed to communicate in a limited way and I think they liked him at first.

'We had a lovely few days in Warsaw and then I took him to see Krakow – one of our most beautiful cities – and

30

we travelled around the country. My sister came with us too. It was a very happy time.

'When we got back to Warsaw everything still seemed to be going well. Tibor and my father were soon very friendly with each other, but when my father asked him about his plans he said he was bored with music. He just wanted to be incredibly rich and live in the sun. "I have a dream of great wealth," he said, "and nothing to do except spend it!"'

'"That's some dream," my father said. He had been in prison under the old political system because he was a member of a banned trade union. Now he works in a hotel. His life hasn't been nearly as exciting as he had planned. Well not so far, anyway.' Malgosia stopped talking and slowly drank her coffee.

'One night I had to go out,' Malgosia started again after a few minutes, 'to my friend Irena's. She was going to get married the next day, so all of her girlfriends, we had organised a party for her. We had a wonderful time. We laughed a lot and I'm afraid to say we drank quite a lot too. So at the end of the party I stayed at Irena's house. I rang my father to say I wasn't coming home. He said that Tibor and my sister had gone out for a drink. I was pleased they were getting on so well. You always want your family to like your boyfriend, don't you?

'Anyway, I woke up very early and because Irena was sleeping soundly, I left the house without disturbing her. I caught an early morning tram. When I got home I let myself in quietly. I wasn't feeling very good, as you can imagine. I hung my coat on its hook. I kicked off my shoes. I made a cup of coffee. I didn't want to wake anyone. But in the end I realised that I was feeling so bad that I would have to go back to bed so I went into the room I shared with my sister ...' Malgosia paused, frowned, and then continued, 'and my sister Anja was there, of course, fast asleep. So was Tibor. Next to her. In her bed. For a moment I didn't recognise him. Or perhaps I didn't want to recognise him.

'"That's nice," I thought, "she's got a boyfriend," and then it hit me and I dropped the cup of coffee I was carrying. It made a terrible noise and coffee went everywhere. Tibor woke up at that point. He looked a bit surprised. Anja opened her eyes too, and when she saw me she let out a little scream, something like "Oh no". And I started screaming too. I mean, I know what Tibor is like, I've always known, ever since I met him. But I thought he had changed, I thought he really loved me. And the one place you feel safe, you know, is in your family. But my sister. My sister! I couldn't believe that she would do that. I couldn't believe he would do that.

'The noise woke my parents, of course, and they came running into the room to see what was happening. Soon everybody was shouting and I said some terrible things. Tibor left later in the morning. And since then it's just been getting worse and worse. Anja and I, we fought all the time, and yesterday I said some unforgivable things to my father.'

'He must have realised you were upset,' I said, to be helpful.

'Yes,' Malgosia replied miserably. 'But I asked him why he loved Anja more than me and why he'd been prepared to fight for his union in the old days but now he wouldn't even stand up for me against my sister. I called her a lot of names. I threw something at her. Then my father threw me out of the house. So, I've come here to you,' she said. 'It's the only place I could think of. I've lost Tibor, I've lost my family, I have no home anymore. What am I going to do?' And she burst into tears.

Much later I put her in my bed, and after she had cried some more she fell asleep, and all night I sat and watched her.

*   *   *

Malgosia and I got married three years later, and I thought I was the happiest man alive. The woman who I worshipped as if she was a god had agreed, after a great deal of persuasion, to become my lover and then, in the end, my wife. For her even second best was better than nothing in the end.

Malgosia's parents and grandparents came for the wedding. (Though her sister Anja didn't – there was still an icy distance between her and Malgosia.) My parents were on their best behaviour too. When they had first met Malgosia they had expressed their concern. My father had even gone so far as to say, 'I don't think she's really your type, son! She'll cause you pain. I'm sure of that!' and I had been terribly offended and we had an argument. But on our wedding day they were all smiles, and I was grateful to them for helping to make it such a special occasion.

I liked my new mother-in-law. She was much calmer than her daughter.

'You must not to blame Malgosia if she is always exciting,' she told me in her rather broken English. 'You must understand. The mix up with that Tibor. And before. It was

33

a difficult time, her childhood, with the politics, police are coming often. She is very romantic now, very . . . What is the word . . . ? Passionate, yes, passionate. But I think you know that already. I think she is lucky, my daughter.' She kissed me on the cheek. 'You will be careful of her?' she asked, and I said yes. That's exactly what I would do. It was such an easy promise to make, such a difficult promise to keep.

The trouble started a few years later. By then our quartet was doing well: Rachel had stopped feeling angry in the end (back in those days at the Academy) and the four of us had stayed together ever since, improving our playing, developing a musical understanding between us that made it all worthwhile. Malgosia's career was going well too. She was getting work in musical shows in the West End. Both of us did some teaching as well and our lives seemed to be very comfortable, although Malgosia often looked bored and we had some days when we hardly spoke to each other. But all marriages are like that, I thought, so I didn't worry very much.

But then one day, when I was practising in the music room, the phone rang. I was just about to put down my viola and go to answer it when I heard Malgosia's voice coming from the kitchen. And for some reason I half listened. I couldn't hear what my wife was saying, of course, but it was a long conversation and sometimes she was silent, but sometimes she talked urgently in a low voice. I nearly went to listen to the conversation properly, to see who it was she was speaking to, but the piece of music I was working on was very difficult, and the quartet were due to play it in a concert next day, so I kept on playing.

After twenty minutes my curiosity got the better of me. I opened the door. As I did so I heard Malgosia say 'goodbye' in a loud and unnatural voice.

I walked into the kitchen.

'Who was that?' I asked.

'Rosemary,' she said.

'That was a long conversation,' I went on, wanting to see what she would say.

'Well yes. We're friends. She's got problems,' Malgosia answered in a bad-tempered kind of way.

'What problems?' I asked, though I knew that Rosemary's husband had left her. I just wanted to see how my wife would answer. I suppose, subconsciously I knew that something was wrong.

'You know, Ted has left her, and she has to look after the children on her own, and he's not giving her enough money. The usual. Look,' she said suddenly, as if a thought had just come to her, 'I'm going for a walk. Do you mind?'

'A walk?' I replied stupidly. 'Why do you want to do that?' Malgosia never went for walks on her own.

'I don't know. I'm just feeling a bit on edge, a bit depressed. About Rosemary, probably, so I'll just go and walk it off.'

'I'll come with you,' I said. I didn't like her to feel sad.

'No,' she answered immediately, 'I'd rather be on my own.' And before I could protest she had walked past me, taken her coat from the hall, and walked out of the house, slamming the door behind her.

When she came back she was calmer. She said she was sorry. She asked me to understand that she was a difficult person sometimes, that was just how she was. I knew that already of course, and I loved her very much and so I said of course I understood.

'Only please,' I said pathetically, 'do think of me sometimes, of how it feels to be me.'

'Poor Derek,' she said, and kissed me. And the next day, when I came home from the concert I had played in with the quartet, Malgosia was waiting for me. She had cooked a special meal and there was an open wine bottle on the kitchen table.

'Why aren't you at the theatre?' I asked, surprised. She was playing in the band for 'The Phantom of the Opera' at that time.

'I have taken a few days off,' she said sweetly. 'Come on Derek darling, sit down and have a glass of wine.'

'You're not working there for a few days?' I asked. 'Why not?'

'Because I need some time to myself. I need to be alone to think about some things.'

'What do you mean "I need to be alone"? How are you going to "be alone"?' I asked her.

'Well, I wasn't going to say this straight away . . .' She sat with her back to me, and spoke in a soft nervous voice '. . . but now that we're talking about it, well, I'm going to go away for a few days. If that's all right.'

I didn't say anything. This was typical of Malgosia. Sudden decisions, surprises, always doing things for herself. It is what I loved about her. It was what caused me pain.

'Look, Derek, I'm sorry. I know you think I'm selfish. I know I cause you trouble sometimes. But I couldn't live without you, you know that.'

'I know,' I answered, believing her. I always believed her. 'But what's all this about going away?'

'Just for a few days, that's all. I just want to disappear, be by myself, have time to think.'

'But what about?' I asked again. 'What do you need to think about?'

'Life. My past. My parents. Us. The music. Everything,' she said. 'Everyone needs time on their own sometimes. You're going to Birmingham for two days next week with the quartet. I thought it was just the perfect time.'

'OK, even if I agree with you, where are you going?' I asked.

'I don't know. I haven't decided. Maybe Scotland,' she said dreamily.

And so I let her go. She didn't tell me where she would be staying and she didn't get in touch with me while she was away. But I was out of the house as well so it wasn't too much of a problem. I just thought, 'poor old Malgosia, such a complicated woman, so intense, so special, so different. Of course she needs her "space", her time away. There's nothing wrong with that.'

When she got back she was happier than I had seen her for some time. There was a brightness about her, an excitement, a sparkle in her eyes. She came running into the house and flung her arms around me.

'Oh Derek,' she said, like some actress in a movie (which I suppose is what she was). 'It's so lovely to see you.' She told me she had been in a convent in the north of Scotland, a hidden-away religious order somewhere I'd never heard of. She said she felt much better now, much calmer. She said that many of her doubts about herself were over with. She made me happy.

And so I never asked her where she went. I trusted her.

Looking back I can't believe that I was so naive, but she was so different, so wild and passionate, just as her mother had told me. Her troubled childhood had affected her, that terrible business with Tibor, all that had made her the person she was. I still couldn't believe my luck that she had agreed to marry me even though I knew that I fell far short of her ideal. But in time that thought faded and I learned to be happy.

Ten months later she went away again. Now I realise that it was the same pattern as before (although, at the time I didn't notice). First, a telephone call. Malgosia said it was Rosemary or a musician friend or somebody. I can't remember. Then two days later she suddenly announced that she needed some time on her own again. She seemed troubled. I even wondered if she was ill in some way. But I let her go. Back to that same convent, or so I thought, where they didn't have any telephones (she said) so I couldn't get in touch with her. When she came back she was happy as before, bursting with life, recovered, alive. I thought, again, that these days of reflection were, for her, better than a visit to a psychoanalyst, better than the drugs she might otherwise have taken.

It happened twice more. Each time Malgosia came home a different person and, for a time after she returned, we were as happy as we had been at the beginning of our relationship, before we started arguing, not talking to each other or even, what was worse, being extremely polite.

When she came back from the last trip she brought a new trumpet with her. She said she had come across it in a music shop in Glasgow on her way back. She'd had a few hours before her train left for London. She'd fallen in love with the instrument the moment she'd set her eyes on it,

38

she said. She hoped I didn't mind. She knew I'd understand. It was going to make her playing even better.

I asked to listen to it, but she said 'not yet'. She wanted to get used to it first, practise on it, learn its funny ways and manners. Then I could hear it. I understood how she felt, but I was a bit offended that she wasn't involving me in the strange relationship that every musician has with a new instrument. It was almost as if she was cheating on me. She kept it shut in its case. She had only shown it to me that first time when she arrived back home, and even then she'd just opened the case quickly and let me look inside before shutting it up again.

The new trumpet stayed in the corner of the music room for weeks. Once, I don't know why, I tried to open it to have a look inside but it was locked. When I heard Malgosia practising (which she had started to do with the door closed) it sounded the same as usual to me, as if she was using her old instrument.

And then one night, about three and a half weeks after she had returned from that last trip, I came home, but Malgosia wasn't in the house, and there was a message on the computer from Tibor. And while I was trying to understand why Tibor was in contact with her after all this time, and while I was trying to absorb the fact that my wife had probably gone to Rio de Janeiro without telling me, there was a knock at the door and two policeman were standing there.

'We just want to ask Mrs Armstrong a few questions,' they said. Before I knew it, they were in my house, and because Malgosia wasn't there, they questioned me instead.

# Chapter 5   *Deciding on priorities*

'Have you ever been to Scotland, sir?' asked one of the policemen, a middle-aged man who obviously ate and drank more than was good for him.

'Scotland?' I said stupidly. As I think I've already said, I wasn't thinking very clearly.

'Yes, sir,' the man said, 'it's that place just north of England. Have you heard of it?'

'Oh, very funny,' I replied. How could he be so sarcastic at a time like this?

'Glad you enjoyed my joke, sir,' he said without smiling, 'but what's the answer? Have you ever been to Scotland?'

'Yes, of course,' I replied. 'With my family when I was a child, and I've played in the Edinburgh Festival with my quartet about three times, yes, three times.' We had our first great success there. The Edinburgh Festival is one of Europe's great artistic events.

'When was that, sir? When did you play in the Edinburgh Festival?'

'The last time?' I said. 'About two years ago.'

'So you haven't been to Scotland for two years?' said the other policeman, a younger man with very short hair and a nasty look in his eyes.

'That's right, officer. I've just had this crazy idea,' I said, and then I added, 'If you listen to what I say you won't have to ask me questions more than once. What do you think of that?!'

'Let's get one thing straight,' the short-haired one said, 'you can help us or you can be difficult. If you want to be difficult that's your decision, of course, but we can make your life very uncomfortable. Now, for example, we can have this conversation here in the comfort of your own home. Or better still, we can take you down to the police station and question you there. What do you think of that?'

'I'm sure that won't be necessary,' said the fat policeman. He was obviously the 'nice' one in the pair. 'I'm sure Mr Armstrong will help us in any way he can. Won't you, sir?'

'I suppose so,' I heard myself saying. I just wanted them to go so I could try and decide what to do. Though I already had a pretty good idea.

'Good. That's better. Now then, sir,' the short-haired one went on, 'you say you haven't been to Scotland for two years. What about your wife?'

'Well, yes. She's been a few times. She came up to the festival to hear us play the first time we were there,' I said, remembering how happy we had all been, 'but it's difficult for her to get away from her own work sometimes, so she didn't come with us on the other two occasions we played there.'

'Yes, it must be difficult for her, getting away,' said the unpleasant policeman with a nasty tone in his voice.

'And that's the only time your wife went to Scotland?' the first policeman asked.

'Yes,' I started and then I suddenly remembered. 'I mean no. She's been there a few times. On her own. To get away. You know, to get some personal "space". We all need it sometimes, don't we ...' I stopped. They were both looking at me strangely.

'And when she's been on her own,' the short-haired one said, 'where has she been, exactly?' I thought I heard excitement in his voice.

'She goes to a convent,' I replied, 'a religious order. It's a very private place.'

'I see, sir,' said the first policeman, 'and where would that be, the convent?'

'I don't know,' I said. It suddenly sounded silly, even to me.

'I'm sorry, sir,' said the nasty one, 'what did you say?'

'Look,' I protested, 'I know it probably sounds strange, but Malgos ... my wife, well she is quite a nervous person, so she goes off for a bit of peace and quiet, you know. It's perfectly OK. I trust her completely, you see. She doesn't have to give me the address or anything. I mean why should she, if she wants to get away from it all?'

'Do you know of someone called ...' the overweight policeman glanced down at his notebook. 'Tibor Arkadi?'

Tibor! The shadow in my relationship ever since we had met, ever since Malgosia had turned up at my door at the beginning of my second year at college, her hair wet from the rain, her heart broken by the man who had fooled around with her sister.

'Well, yes,' I replied, trying to stop my voice trembling. 'He was a student with us.'

'And where might that have been?' asked the fat policeman.

'At the Royal Academy of Music,' I answered automatically.

42

'And have you seen him since then?' the short-haired one said.

'No, no I haven't,' I replied truthfully.

'What about your wife?' he went on. 'Has she seen him?'

I hesitated. Two hours ago I would have said 'no, of course not', but that was two hours ago. Since then I'd seen the e-mail. But then again, Malgosia was my wife and if she hadn't told me about Tibor I was sure she wouldn't want me to tell the police.

'Well, sir,' asked the friendly one, 'has she seen him?'

'No, no I'm sure she hasn't,' I replied.

'Well, sir, that's about all then,' said the nasty one suddenly. 'I don't think we need to bother you anymore.' He got up as if to go.

'Excuse me,' I said. 'Can you tell me what this is all about?'

'We'll let you know as soon as we have anything to tell you,' he said. 'Oh by the way, where is she, your wife?'

'She's not here. She's gone away.'

'And where would that be?' said the larger man. 'Not to Scotland, I expect.'

'No,' I said, 'she hasn't gone to Scotland.'

'Did she bring anything back from Scotland ever?' said the younger policeman. 'Anything special?' The older policeman looked as if he was annoyed at the younger man's interruption.

'No,' I said miserably, remembering how she never even brought me back a bottle of Scotch whisky or a tin of shortbread biscuits. But then it suddenly dawned on me. The new trumpet! Oh no! I was beginning to piece things together and, although I wasn't anywhere near the truth yet, I wasn't completely wrong either.

43

'Yes, sir?' the policeman went on. He must have seen the look on my face.

I never had a chance to answer. Suddenly the fat policeman's radio started making noises and when he pressed a button on his chest I heard something like: 'code 94 code 94,' and an address repeated over and over again.

'Sorry, sir, but we have an emergency, we have to go,' said the short-haired one. 'We'll see ourselves out.'

'Code 94 – policeman in trouble,' the older one said. 'You drop what you're doing when you get a code 94.' They both ran from the room. At the door the older one said, 'We'll be back, sir. Tomorrow. To continue our interesting conversation. Don't go anywhere, will you?'

'All right,' I said, and closed the door behind them. Then I ran into the music room. There must be something special about the new trumpet Malgosia had bought. Even if the case was locked I was determined to find out.

But when I got into the music room and looked in the usual place, I realised that I wasn't going to discover anything. Her new trumpet wasn't there. There was just her old one, lying on top of the piano.

\* \* \*

Rosemary was surprised to see me standing outside her front door at half past eleven at night.

'Derek,' she said in amazement. 'What are you doing here?' She looked at the suitcase I was carrying. 'I was just on my way to bed,' she said.

Rosemary, my wife's best friend, is an editor for a big fiction publisher in London. Her husband – her ex-husband by then – was a choreographer. He'd gone off with one of the dancers in a show he was doing, leaving Rosemary broke and depressed. But before he'd left her he'd taken Rosemary to an opening-night party of a musical where Malgosia was playing. The two women had met, got on well immediately, and had become best friends. It helped that Rosemary lived near us, of course.

I quite liked Rosemary too, but she was Malgosia's friend rather than mine. Sometimes when the two of them were talking I felt like an outsider. Sometimes it was even worse and I might just as well have been the enemy.

I could understand why Rosemary was upset of course. Her husband had left her and she was badly hurt. But it didn't seem terribly fair to me. Not all men are the same, surely. I hadn't done anything bad to her. I hadn't even done anything very bad to my own wife, except bore her.

'I'm sorry to turn up like this,' I told her. 'I wouldn't do it under normal circumstances, honestly I wouldn't. But I need your help.'

'If it's about Malgosia, I don't think I can tell you anything,' she said nervously. She hadn't opened the door any wider. 'I mean, I don't think I should.'

'Look, Rosemary, please,' I said. 'Let me in. I'm begging you.'

'Derek,' she replied, starting to close the door. 'I think you'd better go.'

Desperation makes you behave in funny ways. I'm not a violent man or anything, and normally if someone tells me to go, I go straight away. Aggression isn't part of my make up. At least it didn't use to be before all this started. But after the afternoon and evening I'd had, I wasn't going to be put off that easily.

I crashed into the door and when Rosemary tried harder to close it on me I forced my foot inside. And then we fought to see whether she could shut me out or I could force my way in.

I won in the end. I am stronger than she is, and I was more determined. The door crashed open and Rosemary was thrown against the wall of the passageway where she stood, wide-eyed and confused. I shut the door behind me.

'Did you know about this?' I asked her without any introduction.

'Did I know about what?' she replied. She was hardly whispering. She must have thought I was about to attack her or something.

'Oh come on!' I had started shouting, even though I didn't mean to. 'Did you know about Tibor? What has she told you?'

'Please, Derek,' Rosemary said, edging away from me. 'Please don't shout. You'll wake the children. Please, Derek.' She was frightened. My anger disappeared immediately.

'Look, Rosemary, I'm sorry. I'm really sorry. But I am desperate and I do need your help. I think Malgosia's in trouble. The police came and asked me questions about her. Even if you don't want to help me, you must help her.'

'All right, all right. Come in,' she said. 'But just for a moment. I've got a busy day tomorrow. I've got a book to finish. The woman who usually looks after the kids is ill. I don't know what I'm going to do.'

She led me into the kitchen.

'Do you want a drink?' she asked. 'A coffee? A glass of wine?'

'Coffee, please,' I said. 'I think I've had enough wine this evening.'

'Yes,' she said, 'I can see that. You look terrible.'

'Thanks,' I said. I sat down. Now that I had got here I felt suddenly very tired.

'What's this all about?' Rosemary said from over by the sink where she was filling the kettle.

So I told her. I told her about the e-mail message, about Rio de Janeiro and Tibor. I told her about the police and the questions they had been asking me. I told her everything I knew.

She didn't say much. She just listened.

'Why didn't you ring?' I asked her suddenly. 'You said you were going to ring.'

'Yes, I did. I'm sorry,' she said, handing me my coffee, 'but I didn't know what to tell you. I didn't know what I could tell you. It's not really my business, you see, what Malgosia does, what you do. Anyway, I couldn't betray a friend.'

'Rosemary,' I told her, 'you above all people should know what it's like when your husband or your wife starts behaving strangely. Don't you think I have a right to know?'

'Malgosia's my friend,' she replied simply.

'So what was she doing in Scotland? Do you know that?'

'Not exactly, no,' Rosemary said. She was speaking quietly now, sympathetically. 'I do know she met someone up there, and that it made her very happy. I'm sorry, Derek,' she said. She must have seen my face. 'But I don't know who it was. Perhaps it was this Tibor.'

'And you approved of that?' I asked.

47

'Of course not. It's not my style. I told Malgosia so too. But she said she couldn't help it. She said it was like an illness, an addiction, a need she couldn't control. But just lately she started talking differently.'

'How do you mean?' I asked, feeling suddenly frightened.

'She was really thoughtful about something. She wouldn't say what. She just said that something was going to happen, that she was going to have to do something, and that she might have to leave. She said that she didn't know if it was the right thing to do or not but she wouldn't give me any details. What could I say? I thought she was just being silly. I told her to make a decision. She should either choose you or whoever the other person was. Then she wouldn't have anything to worry about. And she said that might have been possible once, but that now things were much more complicated. I think – well, I thought then – that she was being asked to do something she didn't really want to, something like that.'

'You're going to follow her, aren't you?' Rosemary said a little later, because it was obvious.

'Yes,' I replied, 'of course. What else can I do? But the police will be back and if Malgosia really is in trouble they'll keep me here to ask me more questions. That's why I came to you. They won't look for me here. I need to stay the night. Is that all right. I'll be gone tomorrow.'

'Poor old Derek,' Rosemary said. 'Yes, it's all right. I hope you find her. I hope she's all right.'

*   *   *

I didn't sleep much that night on Rosemary's sofa. And when I did finally manage to sink into unconsciousness it

48

seemed only a few minutes before I woke to find Rosemary's two small children looking at me curiously.

I crawled out of the sleeping bag she had lent me and climbed into my clothes. I found Rosemary in the kitchen, pouring cornflakes into the children's bowls.

'There's coffee in the pot,' she said. I drank a black coffee, no sugar. Then I told her I would be going in a couple of hours.

'Which airport?' she asked. 'What flight are you taking?'

'I don't think I'm going to tell you,' I replied, looking up from my cup. 'If the police come here I'd much rather you didn't know anything.'

I left at nine forty-five. Rosemary came to the door.

'Derek,' she said standing on the front doorstep, her expression much warmer than it had been the night before, 'I hope you find what you want.'

'So do I,' I told her.

'And Derek,' she said, 'I know you think I don't like you, but I do really. It's just that, well I thought Malgosia was my friend. Will you forgive me?'

'There's nothing to forgive,' I said.

'Dear Derek,' she said softly and kissed me on the cheek before going back into the house and closing the door behind her.

\* \* \*

When I left Rosemary's house, I went straight to the quartet's practice room; only Rachel had arrived.

'Hello Dee,' she said. She had been calling me that for some time now. 'Why have you got your suitcase with you? Where's the viola?'

49

'I can't do it.' I said. 'I can't do this practice. Not today. Or this week. I don't know for how long. For some time.' I felt really bad about this. I knew I was letting my friends down.

'What? What are you saying?' Rachel asked.

'I'm afraid I've got to go away for a bit,' I repeated. 'There's something I've got to do.'

'What?' she said. A look of anger was beginning to appear on her face. What have you "got to do"?'

'I can't explain,' I replied. 'It's personal.'

'It's personal!' she exploded. 'What on earth does that mean? What about the quartet? That's personal. Well, it is to me anyway. What are we going to do if you just disappear? Where are you going anyway?'

'Brazil.'

'Brazil?! Whereabouts?'

'Rio de Janeiro, I think,' I said unhappily.

'Derek,' Rachel said, her voice softening, 'Derek, what's the matter? Something's wrong isn't it? Something's terribly wrong.'

'I wish I could tell you,' I said to her. And I really did. Rachel was probably my best friend. We had forgotten the problems of our youth. Now we seemed to work well together and I found her company relaxing. It was easy to laugh with her, it was easy to be ordinarily happy, it was a joy to see her smile.

Carl walked into the practice room.

'Hello,' he said. 'Everything OK?' Then he looked from one to the other of us, and saw that everything was not all right at all. When I told him I was going away for a bit he didn't say anything for a moment. Then he looked at me and, in a quiet voice, asked, 'How could you? How could you? After all this time?' Then he sat down and his head fell into the front of his large black overcoat.

Matt, on the other hand, was absolutely furious. He went red in the face and started shouting. 'How can you do this to us?' he yelled. 'We're all in this together, we're a team, a family. We're just about to do the most important concerts of our lives and you say you've got to go off to South America because of some personal problem – with Malgosia, I suppose. I think you'd better decide where your priorities are. That's what I think. Jesus!' He finished and walked across the room to stare out at a grey February sky.

'Look,' I said, 'Matt, Carl, Rachel, all of you, I wouldn't do this if I knew of any other way. Honestly. I'm really, really sorry.'

'You will be,' Carl said, 'if you come back and find someone else sitting in your place.'

'I'm sorry,' I said, a chill settling on my heart at the thought of what I was risking. 'I really am. You don't know how sorry I am.' They were all standing there now looking as miserable as I was. What could I do?

I walked out into the street and shouted for a taxi.

'Where to, mate?' the driver asked me.

'Heathrow,' I told him, 'Heathrow Airport.'

# Chapter 6 *Breathtaking views*

From the rooftop terrace of my hotel, high up above the twenty-fifth floor, the view of Rio de Janeiro was breathtaking. Like everybody else I had seen pictures, films, TV programmes and travel magazines which featured this most famed of South American holiday destinations: but nothing had prepared me for the dramatic beauty of the place. The sky was bright blue and the sun was hot on my face.

Below me, I could see the long curved strip of Copacabana beach. Even from this height it was possible to make out groups of people playing volleyball, or lying on the sand, and the cars moving up and down the seafront seemed to glow with heat and excitement. Over to the right a rocky cliff rose up above the beach limiting the extent of the almost white sand, while to the left the extraordinary lump of Sugar Loaf Mountain, a great big iced-lolly of a rock, almost seemed to be smiling at me, inviting me to visit. Or perhaps that's just how it seems now, looking back. I could see a cable car hanging from the wires that snaked towards its summit.

Out here in the bright glare of the sun I still felt miserable, but already it was a different kind of misery, more immediate, more alive, like a sharp pain, with the promise of relief. There was something almost exciting about it.

On the roof of the Rio Atlantica Hotel there was a large swimming pool, poolside chairs and a bar. I had come up here last night when I had arrived and now, even though I knew I had a lot to do, I couldn't resist it. And so, an hour after breakfast, here I was, all English and white-skinned, wearing my swimming trunks, ready for a swim.

The water was warm when I dived in and for a few minutes I swam around just enjoying the luxury of it all. Not much more than twenty-four hours ago I had been sitting in my house with two English policemen asking me awkward questions on the other side of the world. Now here I was in the bright sunshine, and already some of my troubles seemed thousands of miles away. This was another world, a world without musicians and disappearances, a world where Malgosia and I . . .

Malgosia! How could I have forgotten her, even for a minute, even in the warmth of this exciting new place? I opened my mouth in surprise and immediately swallowed a litre of water. I started to cough and swallowed more water. I made my way to the side of the pool, coughing and spluttering.

'Are you all right?' said a cheerful, singing voice which glittered like the sun on the water.

'Yes,' I coughed, 'I'm fine,' and coughed some more.

'Here,' said the new voice, heavily accented, warm and friendly, 'let me give you a hand.'

I looked up, straight into the sun. I screwed up my eyes. There was a woman standing at the poolside.

I pulled myself out of the pool, still coughing, and flicking my wet hair out of my eyes, I looked at the person who had been talking to me. She was probably a bit younger

53

than me, dressed in a bright green bikini, her skin tanned a dark brown, the thick, black hair falling in tight curls over her shoulders. She had the biggest smile I had ever seen.

'You'd better be careful!' she laughed. 'That white skin of yours is going to burn bright red in the sun – that is if you don't drown first!' I should have been insulted, but she sounded so cheerful that I had to laugh with her.

'I'll be careful,' I said. 'But thanks.'

'I am Sandra,' she said. 'Welcome to Rio. This is your first time?'

'In Rio?' I answered. 'Yes. I'm Derek, by the way, from England.'

'Ah, from England. Queen Elizabeth, Prince Charles, the tragic story of Princess Diana.'

'Well, there's a bit more to it than that,' I said feeling slightly defensive. 'Anyway, where are you from?'

'Me?' said Sandra. 'I am a true Carioca.'

'What's a Carioca?' I said.

'A Carioca is someone from Rio de Janeiro, the most beautiful place in the world. Don't you think?'

'It's difficult to tell,' I said. 'I haven't been to all that many places.'

'Well, anyway,' my new friend continued, 'are you going to buy me a beer?'

'Isn't it a bit early?' I answered.

'It's never too early,' Sandra replied. 'Anyway, you look as if you need one.'

We walked over to the bar. I was amazed at how quickly the water dried on my skin. I ordered two beers.

'So,' said Sandra, taking a sip from her bottle. 'Are you here on holiday?'

'Not really,' I answered, 'not on holiday.'

'So what is this? Business?' she asked.

'No,' I replied, 'it isn't business.' I stopped. I didn't quite know how to explain.

'Are you being mysterious on purpose?' said the beautiful girl beside me, sounding a little annoyed.

'No, I'm sorry, I'm not.' I said. 'It's just that, well, it's a bit difficult to explain why I am here.'

'Try me,' she said, and I suddenly realised that I knew absolutely nothing about her. It was probably just the foreign sky and the fantastic place I was in that had made me talk to her so freely in the first place.

'Look,' I protested, 'I don't know anything about you, anything at all. I know that sounds rude, but . . .'

'Not rude,' she laughed. 'Just rather boring. Still, if you really want to know, my brother's the manager of this hotel and so I can come here any time I want and have a swim in safety.'

'What's wrong with the sea?' I asked.

'Oh nothing, really, but Rio is not always very comfortable. There are some difficult people about. Anyway,' she went on, 'now that you know more about me you can answer my question. Why have you come to Rio?'

'I'm looking for someone,' I said.

'Wow!' she laughed. 'That sounds dramatic. Who are you looking for?'

'My wife.' It sounded so stupid, so humiliating. 'And someone else.'

'Ah,' said my friend, 'she has left you?'

'Yes. No. I don't know.' I had started now and I didn't

know how to stop. And when I had told her just about everything she said nothing for a bit.

'And you really want to find her?' Sandra asked.

'Yes, of course,' I said, 'that's why I'm here.'

'Whatever the consequences?' she insisted.

'Yes, yes, of course.'

'All right,' she said, standing up as if to go, 'meet me in the lobby downstairs in fifteen minutes and I'll take you to see someone. He might be able to help you.'

\*   \*   \*

Oswaldo Morales was a large man with gold rings on his short fingers and an expensive gold watch strapped around his large wrist. He had thin, black hair combed forward across his sweaty skull and his brightly-coloured, short-sleeved shirt was stretched tight across his large stomach. He was smoking the biggest, smelliest cigar I have ever seen and he sat behind a large wooden desk – the kind teachers used to have in their classrooms – which was covered with papers, ashtrays, three dirty coffee cups, and a telephone that must have been at least sixty years old. There were two filing cabinets on his left, with half-open drawers. An old air-conditioning machine which was completely ineffective rattled away noisily behind him.

'Sandra,' he cried, taking his feet off the desk and getting up awkwardly. 'How are you my love? How nice to see you!' He edged his way around the desk and kissed her on the cheek. 'My,' he said, 'you are looking beautiful, as always.'

'And you are looking, well, the same as usual too!' Sandra said.

'Yes, I know,' replied the fat man, 'it's terrible. But what can I do? I don't have any time for exercise, and anyway I hate it. And the only other possibility is to cut down on the amount I eat and drink and frankly, my dear, that is too terrible to think of.'

His accent was more difficult to understand than Sandra's. I wondered if they were speaking English just for my benefit.

'Anyway,' he went on, 'I suppose this is the Englishman you told me about when you rang.' He smiled at me.

'Yes, yes, that's me,' I replied. The room was very hot and the smoke made it difficult to breathe. Maybe it was the jet-lag but I was feeling rather ill.

'And you want me to find someone for you, I think?' he said, standing close. 'Your wife, I think. Is that right Mr, er . . . ?'

'Armstrong,' I said, 'Derek Armstrong. Can you find her? I mean, are you any good?'

'Listen here, Derek Armstrong,' said the large man sounding more amused than offended, 'I can find anyone if they're in this city. It may take some time, and it may take money – though I'm not very good at collecting money as you can see – but I always get there in the end. By the way, Mr Armstrong, what do you do when you're at home?'

'I'm a musician, a viola player,' I replied.

'A musician eh? I could have been a musician too. Why I could be that Italian, what's his name, Luciano Pava-something – if I had a voice, that is,' and he slapped his stomach and laughed.

The thing I found out about Oswaldo is that when he laughed, really laughed, everybody else ended up laughing too. He was cheerful, disorganised, dangerous and really good fun to be with. Over the next few days we became firm friends, I think, though he was only one more strange person in this strange, extraordinary land I was in, a land with hidden dangers and many surprises.

'Now then,' he said, when we had all stopped laughing, 'it is time we got down to details. Why do you think your wife is in Rio de Janeiro? Perhaps she is somewhere else? Are you sure that she is in Brazil?'

'Pretty sure,' I said, and I told him about the e-mail on the computer. I told him about Tibor, about the old days when we were music students, about the stories from Poland. I told him the story of my life. I told him that my wife had disappeared and that the police had come looking for her.

When I had finished nobody said anything for a minute. Sandra lit a cigarette, adding to the unbearable fog in the hot room.

'Well, well,' Oswaldo said finally, 'and if I find your wife and this Tibor, what then?'

'I haven't the slightest idea,' I told him, 'I haven't really got that far.'

'All right. All right. But you are here. That is all I need to know. For the moment you've given me quite a lot to go on. Do you have a photo of your wife with you? That would be most helpful.'

I pulled my wallet from my back pocket and took out two small pictures of Malgosia, the kind you get in those photo booths at stations and airports.

'Will these do?'

'She is beautiful, your wife,' Oswaldo sighed dreamily.

'This is what I'll do,' he announced suddenly. 'I'll start making enquiries at the airport, and I'll talk to some of my musical contacts. Maybe this Tibor person has been involved in music here if he was a music student all those years ago. But with your English police getting all interested in your wife's movements, my nose tells me ...' he tapped the end of his nose with his finger, 'that this doesn't have much to do with music at all. Still, we shall see. I will contact you in twenty-four hours when I have found out something. Now go back to your hotel. Sandra, this poor man looks as if he will pass out right here in my office and then we will have to carry him home! Take him away.'

At the door, I looked back at the large private detective. He was sitting in his chair again, leaning back, his hands behind his head, staring at the ceiling.

'So, what did you think of Oswaldo the Cuban?' Sandra asked me as we drove fast through the streets.

'Cuban?' I replied. 'I assumed he was from here.'

'Well he is, really. All the foreigners who come here, if they stay long enough, they become Cariocas too. Oswaldo is one of us now. And by the way, don't be fooled. He may look extraordinary, but he's good at his job.'

'Can I ask you a question?' I said to her as the taxi pulled up outside the hotel.

'Of course,' said my beautiful companion.

'Why are you helping me like this?' I asked her. It had been puzzling me all day.

'What, you think I am trying to pick you up? You think this is a "pull"?'

'No, no I didn't mean that,' I said, embarrassed, and wishing that I hadn't asked. 'But you've been so nice to me.'

'It's my day off. I was curious, that's all. I like, what do you say, being nosy. I enjoy talking to English-speaking people. Anyway,' she laughed, 'what makes you think you're such a good prospect anyway, one jet-lagged British man, a little sunburnt already, who's miserable because he can't find his wife. Now tell me, what's so special about that?'

We were inside the hotel lobby now, where the air-conditioning worked fine.

'Look,' said Sandra, 'I can tell you're tired. Why don't you go up to your room, have a shower, go to bed and sleep for a couple of hours, then what do you say, we can go and have dinner. What do you think of that?'

'I think that's wonderful,' I said sleepily, and waving goodbye I walked over to the lift and made my way to my room.

I woke up refreshed. Looking out of the window I saw Copacabana in the evening light, and for a moment I felt happy. But only for a moment.

The telephone rang in my room and I answered it. It was Sandra waiting for me down in the lobby. When I stepped out of the lift she was there with another man, about my own age.

'This is Paul,' she said. 'A friend. I thought you'd like to have a friend, a colleague.'

'Hello,' said Paul in a recognisably British accent, which surprised me because from his brown skin and cheerful clothes I would have assumed that he was from Rio.

'Paul's one of the ones I told you about,' Sandra laughed. 'An adopted Carioca. He's been here too long. He'll probably never go back!'

'What do you do here?' I asked him as he walked towards the entrance.

'Teach English,' he said, 'I came out here on a one-year contract and I've sort of stayed.'

'You must like it here,' I told him.

'Yes and no. I mean, of course I do. It's the most exciting place I've ever lived, but it drives me crazy too.'

'Come on,' Sandra said to the two of us and we got into a taxi. Twenty minutes later we were in a cable car, swaying upwards towards the summit of *Päo de Azucar* – Sugar Loaf Mountain. Looking down made me feel distinctly nervous.

'Is this thing safe?' I asked.

'Of course it is, don't be such a baby!' Sandra laughed at me. 'Just think of the view you are going to have.'

She was right. From the restaurant at the top of the mountain we could see out over to Santos Dumont airport with planes taking off towards us every few minutes. For a moment it was worrying, but each time the planes turned to the left before they got to Sugar Loaf Mountain and disappeared into the night.

'The *ponte aerea*, air bridge,' Paul said. 'Backwards and forwards to São Paulo. Planes leave every fifteen minutes.'

I enjoyed that meal. The view was fantastic and the company was excellent. Sandra was beautiful and funny and Paul was good company, kind and agreeable.

'I came here because my wife left me,' he told me at one stage, 'so I suppose we have something in common. But at least she didn't just disappear, I knew where she'd gone to.'

'Was it bad? I mean difficult for you?' I asked him.

'At the time it was terrible, yes, but I got over it in the

61

end. Time, you know. And Brazil, one of the greatest countries on earth. And people like Sandra here.'

'Are you two . . . ?' I asked. I had been puzzled by their relationship.

'Oh no. Once, perhaps, eh Sandra?'

'We're just good friends,' Sandra said definitely.

Paul was about to say something, but then there was a ringing sound. Sandra reached into her handbag, pulled out a mobile phone and answered it.

'Don't you just hate those things?' Paul said. 'Unless they're yours, of course.' He grinned, showing me the phone strapped to his belt. 'You've got to have one of these here. I mean, apart from the classes I give at the Institute, I do private classes so I have to keep in touch with my students.'

Sandra talked briefly into the phone in Portuguese. Then she listened for a couple of minutes before pressing a little red button to switch her mobile off.

'That was Oswaldo,' she said, looking at me. 'He thinks he's found your "Tibor". He wants to know what you want to do now.'

# Chapter 7    *Voices in the distance*

'Tell me again where we're going,' I said to Oswaldo, as we drove along by the sea.

'*Angra dos Reis,*' Oswaldo replied, swerving to avoid two motorcyclists who suddenly appeared on our right. 'Playground of the rich. Well, some of it is anyway. It's on an inland sea. People say it's beautiful. They have holiday homes out there.'

'You don't sound as if you like it very much,' I said, trying not to watch the road in front of us. Since my companion didn't seem particularly interested in it, I felt I shouldn't be either.

'Oh it's all right, I suppose,' he laughed. 'But me, I prefer cities, lots of people, cars, noise, bars, all that kind of thing. I need to be surrounded by people, a lot of people, and to feel them, hear them living their noisy complicated lives all around me. That's why I do this job, I suppose. It gives me an excuse to poke my nose into other people's business, find out what they're doing and why, find out who they are. God, I love the life I lead!' He dug me in the side with his elbow and for one scary moment he only had one hand lightly on the steering wheel. For what seemed like hours he was looking at me, not the road. He rolled down the window and threw out the stub of his cigar. We travelled on in silence and I wondered what we would find at the end of our journey.

* * *

'We're in luck,' Oswaldo had said when I talked to him from my room after Sandra and Paul had dropped me back at the hotel. 'I think I've found this Tibor guy so, if you're right, we can probably find your wife too.'

'What do you mean?' I asked. 'Where is he? How did you find him?'

'Hey, wait a minute!' Oswaldo's large voice bellowed down the phone line. 'Not so fast, OK? Just calm down.'

'OK, OK, but just explain.'

'Sure. Well, I went off to the airport like I told you I was going to. I took those photos of your wife, the ones you gave me in my office. And I started by checking all the direct flights from London two days before you arrived. You were right, by the way.'

'Right?' I replied, wishing he'd get on with his story. 'What about?'

'She used her maiden name to travel. She didn't buy a ticket as Malgosia Armstrong, but as Malgosia Kowalewska. She came in on a British Airways flight. And luckily, one of the airport policemen who was keeping an eye on the baggage hall is a friend of mine. We've done each other some favours in the past.'

'And?'

'Well this man, Reinaldo, he noticed your wife. The red hair, he said, was beautiful. He couldn't take his eyes off her. She reminded him of an actress he was especially keen on. When the doors opened he saw her go through to the crowd of people there. And out there – you're not going to like this bit ...'

64

'Go on,' I said through clenched teeth. 'Go on, Oswaldo, please.'

'All right. She went up to a man waiting there and, my friend says, she flung her arms round him. He remembered that particularly because he thought how lucky the guy was. But it didn't surprise him because this guy was always lucky. A man with powerful friends. Someone the police knew a lot about, but someone they'd never managed to pin anything on even though he was a real bad guy.'

'So who was he?' I asked, knowing the answer perfectly well but hoping against hope that it wasn't him. I could see my wife throwing herself into his arms. I wished the picture of the meeting Oswaldo had just described wasn't so clear in my mind.

'He was Tibor Arkadi, as you suspected. So then I think to myself – find out where this Tibor is and we've found Mrs Armstrong. And the best bit is, I didn't even have to go looking for information about where he lives, because everyone in the police force knows where he is, Reinaldo told me. So now I know where we will probably find your wife.'

'Where? Where is he?'

'About two hours' drive from Rio. I'm going to go out there tomorrow morning. I'll be back in the afternoon with some definite news.'

'I'm coming with you,' I told him immediately, without thinking about it.

'That's not a good idea,' Oswaldo said, sounding suddenly serious. 'My friend told me about this Tibor you see. He's a very dangerous man, very dangerous. People who come into contact with him have died, Reinaldo says, and I believe him. Now listen, I'm used to that kind of thing. It's my job. But you . . .'

'I'm coming,' I repeated. 'If you ever want me to pay you, I'm coming.' It was the only thing I could think of to persuade him.

'You can only come,' Oswaldo sighed down the end of the phone line, 'if you promise to do exactly what I tell you to do.'

And now here we were, speeding along the road to find my beautiful wife in the arms of Tibor the ex-conductor who, according to the stories Reinaldo had told the Cuban detective, had added danger, smuggling and murder to the list of his charms, and I didn't know if I was more scared of Oswaldo's driving or of what we were going to see.

*    *    *

'There!' Oswaldo said, pointing through the trees at the house below us, 'that's the one. That's Tibor's place.'

It was a large bungalow, sticking out of the steep hillside which went down to the water, the inland sea. At the bottom of the slope I could see steps leading down to a jetty where two powerful-looking speedboats were tied up. On three sides of the house there was a large wooden terrace looking out over the sea. I could see other houses on the curving hillside to the right and the left. The inland sea stretched away into the distance between high hills. It was a scene of great beauty. It was quiet too. Occasionally a snatch of conversation from one of the houses came to us on the light wind, or the sound of a car in the distance. Otherwise it was very peaceful.

At least we thought it was, but then, behind us, we heard

the sound of a plane getting nearer and nearer. I looked behind me and there it was, a small seaplane, painted dark blue with golden rays on its wings, flashing over our heads so low you could almost touch it.

'Look!' Oswaldo said. 'It's going to land.' We watched as it came down, cutting a great white scar in the water, before turning round and heading back towards the wooden jetty below Tibor's house. When it got near its destination the engine was switched off and the plane drifted in towards us. Two men got out, and walked towards the house.

Below us three other men walked out from the house on to the terrace and looked over the rails. Two of them wore white suits and face masks, like something from a science fiction film. They were carrying cases and a strange-looking machine. Then the third man, the one in normal clothes, turned round and I caught sight of his face – for the first time in more than ten years.

'That's him!' I cried, shocked despite the fact that I was seeing what I had expected to see. 'That's Tibor. Even after all this time I recognise him. He looks the same, a bit fatter –'

'Quiet,' Oswaldo hissed, 'you want them to hear us, to see us?'

One of the men with Tibor looked up at that point, and for a moment I thought we had been discovered. But then he turned back to say hello to the two men who had arrived on the plane. They all started to talk urgently. Then Tibor and one of the new arrivals went back into the house while the white-suited men walked towards the plane.

Oswaldo and I crawled down the hill, keeping out of sight, until we were much nearer the house. We could hear a conversation, some shouting. And then suddenly I heard a voice I was sure I recognised, a female voice, Malgosia's voice. That was enough for me. I got up from behind the tree we were using to hide and started running down the hill.

Before I knew what was happening I'd been hit by something like an express train from behind and I fell to the ground with a surprisingly fast Oswaldo on top of me, his big, plump hand covering my mouth to stop me from crying out.

'You crazy Englishman!' he hissed. 'What the hell's the matter with you?' He took his hand away from my mouth.

'I heard Malgosia's voice,' I managed to say, 'I'm sure of it.'

'Yes,' he replied in a whisper, 'maybe you did, but you're not going to solve any problems by just going in there and asking to see her, are you? Oswaldo's nose says that would land us both in a lot of trouble, a great deal of trouble. It will be much better if we just wait and watch, watch and wait. Then we can decide what to do. So you stop behaving like a lovesick frog and do what I tell you. That was the agreement, wasn't it?'

'Yes,' I gasped, wishing he'd remove his great weight from my legs, 'yes, but . . .'

'No buts,' he hissed urgently, 'look.'

Still lying on the ground, I looked at the terrace. Tibor had come back out of the house with another white-suited man who was carrying something heavy, something large, something with long, red hair. And then I saw Malgosia's head fall back as they started down the steps that led to the jetty.

I am not cut out for heroism or dramatic gestures. I'm a viola player. I love music, I love compromise. I'm even a bit boring. That's why I probably behave a bit stupidly in dramatic situations, whether at Rosemary's front door or on a Brazilian hillside. This time there was no stopping me.

'Malgosia!' I cried, 'Malgosia!' and ran down the hillside. They'd heard me now. Tibor turned round and looked to see where the noise was coming from. The other man stopped. Two more men ran out on to the terrace and looked up. They pulled out guns.

'Malgosia!' I cried again, and I saw her raise her beautiful head and I thought I heard her say 'Derek, Derek, please help me!' But then there was a great bang and something hit me hard on the side of my head. I felt my legs go weak and the day went all dark on me. I heard running feet and more shouting, but now the noises seemed to be getting further and further away and then, suddenly, there was complete silence.

*   *   *

Strange noises. Voices in the distance. Footsteps going up and down somewhere near, echoing on a stone floor. There were unfamiliar smells too. I seemed to be floating in a great black sea, cut off from some other world just the other side of the ocean.

'Derek,' I heard a voice say, thousands of miles away, 'Derek, can you hear me?'

'He's still unconscious,' somebody else said. Hadn't I heard that voice somewhere before? I tried to open my eyes, but my eyelids were like anchors stuck in the mud of some deep river.

'Look, I saw his eyelid move,' a third voice said.

'Just wishful thinking,' said the first voice. Then the voices faded and I was back in my silent, black world.

'Mr Armstrong, Mr Armstrong?' This time the voice was nearer. This time I was determined to open my eyes.

I managed to raise the corner of one eyelid with what seemed like a great effort. I was blinded by bright white light and shut it again. There was someone by the side of my bed. My bed? I was in a bed? What on earth was going on? I forced my eye open again, and managed to keep it open for a second longer. I was in some kind of a room with light-green painted walls. I could see someone in a white coat standing next to me.

A white coat! Oh no! There was a picture starting up inside my head, a picture of two spacemen carrying something, carrying something like a sack of potatoes, something with beautiful red hair.

'Malgosia!' I managed to whisper, 'Malgosia!'

'What was that? What did you say?' said the person beside me in a foreign accent. 'What did you say?'

But I had already made too much effort. The comfortable dark was asking for me again. The light faded, the voice disappeared.

\*   \*   \*

The next time I opened my eyes, Sandra was standing there. I blinked in surprise.

'Derek?' she said, her eyes widening in surprise. 'Derek? You're conscious? Derek?'

'What are you doing here?' I managed to say. 'Where am I anyway?'

'Hospital, of course, where else? Oh it's so good to see you conscious. Wait, I'll go and tell the others. Back in a minute! Nurse!' I heard her call as she left the room.

I looked around me. It was a hospital all right. There was a television on one wall, a large window with a view of the hills behind Rio, and light-green walls with nothing on them at all. I looked down at the bed. There were tubes coming out of my arm. I moved my head. Ouch! It hurt. I put my hand up to the pain, but there was a large bandage around my forehead.

'Derek!' a friendly voice said, as Oswaldo came into the room. 'Are you all right? Please say you are all right.'

'I'm all right. I think. My head hurts, Oswaldo,' I replied. It was difficult to talk.

'You remember my name at least,' he laughed. Sandra had come into the room with Paul and a nurse who was soon busy taking my pulse. They were all looking down at me and smiling.

'You all right, old chap?' Paul said.

'Yes, yes I am,' I replied, and I managed to sit up a bit more. 'Can somebody please tell me what I'm doing here?'

So they did. They told me how I'd run down the hill when I'd seen Malgosia being carried to the plane. They told me how I'd shouted her name and how Tibor's men had looked round and how one of them had shot at me.

'You are a lucky Englishman,' Oswaldo laughed. 'You certainly are. I mean, the bullet hit you. Right here!' he said pointing his finger at the side of his head. 'And you should be dead really. But the bullet did not go in.' He used his finger again. 'It went across the side of your head. Made a nasty mess. You were out cold. But it never touched that little brain of yours. Too small I think,' and he laughed.

'How did I get here?' I asked them, to try and give myself time to think.

'You've got Oswaldo to thank for that,' Paul said. 'He just picked you up and ran. He got you away and brought you here. That was four days ago.'

'Yes, and you're too damned heavy,' Oswaldo said, 'so don't ever be that crazy again, OK?'

'OK,' I said weakly. I was beginning to feel bad again and I wanted to go to sleep. But there was something else I had to ask.

'What about Malgosia?' I said, but nobody answered me. 'Come on,' I said. I was desperate to find out before I fell asleep again.

'Derek, this isn't easy,' Sandra said. 'I know you've come all this way to find your wife. You nearly got yourself killed too, but, well this is going to be difficult for you, so I don't really know how to tell you.'

'Tell me what?' I said. I was beginning to feel really awful again.

'She means that your Malgosia isn't here anymore, that's what,' Oswaldo said bluntly. 'She's gone.'

'Gone?' I repeated. 'Gone? Where?'

'She's very ill, I heard,' the detective went on, 'very ill.'

'What do you mean she's very ill? Will somebody explain what's going on?' I asked desperately, 'please.'

'Listen, old chap,' Paul said. 'Oswaldo's been making enquiries. It seems they took your wife up to Recife three days ago. That's in the north east of Brazil. Then they put her on a plane to Europe.'

'Europe?' I said, confused now and terribly worried. 'Where in Europe?'

'Poland,' Sandra said, 'Warsaw. Oswaldo thinks she's gone to Warsaw.'

# Chapter 8    *There's nothing for you here*

Warsaw on a cold, rainy afternoon. The exact opposite of Rio de Janeiro. In Brazil everything had been bright blue. In Warsaw that day as I arrived from the airport, everything was grey, the concrete apartment blocks dull against the wet afternoon, the tower of The Palace of Culture, that old communist monument, disappearing into the damp clouds. Yet I loved Poland. I had always been happy here. Malgosia's family had made me welcome the first time I had come. Even Anja, the one who had betrayed her sister, had been polite, though between her and Malgosia there was an icy formality.

When Malgosia and I had been to visit her family they had shown me the old parts of the city; they'd taken me to Krakow and Gdansk, driving over the long roads of this proud country with its unbeaten spirit, keeping its identity despite the efforts of one foreign power after another over the long course of history to squash its character. It made me realise where Malgosia got her bright-eyed intelligence and her deep dark passion. Everyone I met had always been friendly and I had felt at home.

Not this time, though. Now I was in a taxi, unhappy and confused, my head still bandaged, my mind trying to come to terms with all that had happened to me over the last week, my body tired and hurting, that terrible plane smell in my hair and on my clothes. And I was desperately worried too, worried about what my new Brazilian friends had told me, worried about what I would find in Warsaw.

The taxi stopped outside Malgosia's parents' apartment block. I paid the driver in the zlotys I had changed at the airport and rang the bell. A voice came through the intercom, a voice so like Malgosia's that just for a moment I was fooled.

'Malgosia,' I said hopefully, 'it's Derek.'

'Derek,' said the voice that I suddenly knew wasn't Malgosia at all, 'Derek, why have you come?'

'Where's Malgosia?' I shouted into the machine. 'Let me in, Anja, please.'

'All right,' said the tinny voice at my ear, 'I suppose you'll have to come up.' The buzzer sounded and I pushed open the door. I took the lift up to the fourth floor. When I stepped out into the corridor I saw that the door to the flat was open. I walked inside. Anja was standing there waiting for me, her arms folded. Her hair was cut short. She wore heavy black glasses. She watched me as I struggled in with my suitcase. She didn't look welcoming at all.

'What on earth are you doing here?' was the first thing she said, and then, almost without taking breath, 'My God, what's happened to you? You look absolutely terrible.'

'I feel terrible, all right?' I replied angrily. 'My wife's run off with someone else, I've been questioned by the police, I've travelled halfway round the world, I've been shot at and nearly killed. Now my wife's supposed to be very ill and I don't know why, or where she is, but I know it's pretty damn serious. So of course I look terrible. I've just about had as much as I can take, all right?'

'Poor old Derek,' she said nastily. 'Am I supposed to feel sorry for you?'

'I don't care whether you're sorry for me or not,' I told her. 'I just want to know where my wife is.'

'Oh, all right,' she said. 'You'd better come in. Would you like a vodka or something? I think you're going to need it.' She led me into the kitchen, took a bottle from the freezer and poured a small measure into a glass.

'Go on,' she said, 'it'll do you good.'

'Well, it certainly can't make me feel worse than I do already.' I took the glass from her and emptied it in one swallow. She filled my glass again.

'Aren't you going to have any?' I asked her. She wasn't hostile any more. She looked lost, like a child.

'I don't think so,' she whispered. 'I've had quite a lot already.'

It suddenly occurred to me that the apartment was very empty. When I'd been there before there were always people around: Malgosia's parents, her grandmother and grandfather, her brothers.

'Where is everybody?' I said.

'At the hospital,' she answered in a flat, toneless voice, 'at the hospital. They're all at the damned hospital.' She had started to cry.

'Anja,' I said with increasing terror, 'Anja, for God's sake, tell me what's going on.'

'My sister's dying. That's what going on. Maybe she's already dead. And I'm not there.'

'Why not?' I shouted at her, 'why not?'

'Because I don't dare. Because I can't bear it. Because she was my best friend before Tibor.'

'But that was years ago,' I told her. 'You must have got over that by now.'

'Oh, you fool!' she replied, her eyes suddenly bright flames, almost unable to get her words out. 'Tibor and I ... when he was in Europe, every time he came here ... for years ... and then she took him away from me. She took him back. And now she's dying and I can't bring myself to go and see her. God I hate this life!' She reached for another glass and filled it with the ice-cold vodka. She drank it quickly and had another. And another.

'If you want to go and join the party,' she sneered, her cruel look back again, 'you'd better go to the Central Hospital. But hurry now. You don't want to miss the show.'

\* \* \*

They all looked up when I went in. Malgosia's mother smiled a brief little smile and then turned back again to look through a window at a pale figure lying on a bed behind the glass. It was Malgosia, her waxen features white against the flaming red of her hair.

'Malgosia,' I whispered stupidly. She wouldn't have been able to hear me anyway. 'Malgosia, what's the matter?'

'Nothing is the matter any more,' her father said, turning towards me. His eyes were full of tears. 'You're too late, Derek. Where have you been?'

It took a bit of time for his words to sink in. It took me time to realise that Malgosia couldn't hear me in there. It took me time to realise that after all my journeying I had finally found her and it wouldn't do me any good at all.

I don't know how long I stood there in that room with her family. I was too tired to feel anything, too shocked to understand what had happened, too alone to feel any warmth from the people around me. It was as if a hand of ice had gripped me and was slowly freezing all the life out of my body.

I might have gone on standing there for ever, but Malgosia's mother came up to me.

'Come on, Derek,' she said, taking me by the arm, 'there's nothing we can do here. We'd better leave her now. Come back with us. There's a lot we need to talk about, though none of it really matters anymore.'

We walked out of the hospital. We got into the family car and drove back through the streets of Warsaw in silence.

*   *   *

When we got back to the apartment Anja was nowhere to be seen. Nobody mentioned her absence. The vodka bottle on the kitchen table was empty.

Somebody made some coffee. We all went into the lounge. We sat down in a black silence that seemed to suck the air out of the room. I felt as if I couldn't breathe. Instead of the questions I wanted to ask there was a blank space in my brain where nothing moved, nothing was happening.

Malgosia's father managed to ask his questions, though.

'What kind of a husband do you call yourself?' was his first effort. 'What kind of a husband that lets this happen?'

'Jacek, please,' her mother stopped him, and then said something quickly in Polish, but it didn't seem to calm the unhappy man.

'I asked him a question,' he insisted, in English again, 'so the least he can do is give me a reply.'

I looked up at his face, all twisted with grief. 'I'm sorry,' was the only thing I could think of to say. 'I'm sorry. But I don't understand. I don't understand anything.'

'You don't know why she was in Brazil? You don't know how she managed to get poisoned?' her father asked angrily, his words like gun shots in the tense silence. He had come to stand over me and I could smell the cigarette smoke on his breath.

'Poisoned?' I repeated. I hadn't the slightest idea what he was talking about.

'You didn't know? You didn't know about this?' Malgosia's mother said.

'Please,' I said to her, to all of them in that room. 'I don't think I can take any more of this. I don't know anything about poison. The last time I saw Malgosia, in London I mean, there was nothing wrong with her at all. Except that she was about to leave me and I didn't realise it. And now, well, my God, I just, you see ...' I was having difficulty getting my words out.

'Look,' I told them, since things had gone way too far for me to worry about my pride any more, 'Malgosia left me, all right. She left me to go and join Tibor. Remember him!'

'That bastard!' her father said. 'Hasn't he done enough damage in this family!'

The outside door opened and slammed shut. Anja came into the room.

'The perfect time,' I heard her mother mutter under her breath.

'What?' said Malgosia's sister, obviously drunk. 'Have I missed something? Why aren't you all at the hospital? With

78

my sister. Who I love,' she screamed and started to cry. Her grandmother went to her then and started to talk to her in a low quiet voice. When she told her that her sister was dead Anja started up a low terrible moaning which seemed to go on and on. I wished she would just stop. Even when her father made me go with him into the kitchen we could still hear it, (the inhuman noise of someone who was going to feel guilty for ever.)

But I had other things to worry about. Because what Malgosia's father told me was that my wife had died, in the end, bleeding unstoppably, completely unable to breathe, both typical symptoms of someone who had been poisoned by some form of nerve gas, some kind of chemical agent.

'Nerve gas?' I repeated stupidly.

'Yes. Though they still have to do more tests. They haven't been able to identify what type it was yet. All the doctor will say is that he thinks she must have been exposed to some deadly chemical a few days ago. That's his guess anyway.'

'A few days ago,' I said, still without understanding. 'Brazil.'

'And you know nothing about this?' her father asked, looking at me suspiciously with eyes red from weeping.

'No, no, honestly. Look, I'm just trying to absorb what you're telling me. I'm trying to come to terms with what's happened, and to tell you the truth, I'm not doing very well. I'm not doing very well at all.' I desperately wanted to go on talking, drinking coffee, vodka, anything to deaden the pain I was feeling, but suddenly I could do nothing. I felt my legs go from under me, and yet again, blackness washed over me like a wave and I passed out.

*　*　*

The funeral was as bad as a funeral could be; grey rain coming at us almost horizontally from a grey cold sky, the voice of the priest at the graveside taken away from us by a bitter wind, the tears of the mourners invisible in the wet cold. I had recovered some of my physical health, but the colour of my mind was the colour of the sky and I watched the ceremony with an uninvolved kind of despair. When it was over, we all went back to a hotel near the family flat and drank tea and vodka. Some of Malgosia's friends from school had come and they tried to talk to me, to sympathise, but only two of them could speak English, and I wasn't really listening anyway. I had run out of things to say to my in-laws, my ex-in-laws, I suppose, and they didn't seem to know what to say to me.

Anja walked up to me, dressed in black, a black hat covering her face, black glasses hiding her bruised eyes, almost black themselves from so much weeping. She was swaying slightly, a cigarette in one hand, a glass in the other.

'And now what?' she said in a slurred voice. 'What are you going to do now, brother-in-law, the one nobody ever fought over?'

'Anja,' I managed to reply, 'I'm sorry for everything that has happened, I'm sorry you are so hurt and God knows I'm feeling sorry for myself. So the last thing I need is for you to come up to me now and be so damned horrible. Just leave me alone. Please.'

'There's nothing for you here anymore,' she said drunkenly, like a spoiled child. 'Go home, Derek, go home.'

And in the end it seemed like good advice, though without Malgosia I didn't really have a home anymore. Still, I didn't belong here, not now. The next day I caught a flight back to London.

It was a bumpy journey, with turbulence almost all the way. Most of the time I half slept as the plane bounced through the skies, seeing horrible images in my half dreams, images of hospitals and speedboats, beaches and bodies, Malgosia and Tibor in a terrible musical dance of death across the glassy surface of the water. And then, just before we landed, I seemed to be with my quartet again, Rachel smiling at me on my right, Carl and Matt on my left and when I woke up as the plane turned into its final approach to Heathrow I was actually smiling.

But not for long. The truth came home to me almost immediately as the British Airways Boeing 767 went through its final descent, and I sank back into the despair I had fallen into the moment I saw Malgosia's body lying behind the glass in that hospital room. I didn't think, then, that anything, least of all music, would ever pull me out of that.

When the plane landed it taxied away towards the terminal building, but then, unexpectedly, it came to a stop. The captain's voice came over the loudspeakers.

'This is your captain again, ladies and gentlemen. I'm sorry we've stopped, but we've got some visitors who want to come aboard. I'm sure it won't take very long and then we'll make our way over to our landing gate as soon as possible.'

At the front of the plane the flight attendants were opening the door. I looked out of the window and saw steps being driven up to the plane, followed by a police car, its blue light flashing in the darkness. Two men ran up the steps, and when they entered the plane I knew at once who they were. They made straight for my seat.

'Mr Armstrong,' said the older of the two policemen who had visited me two weeks ago in London. 'I am glad to see you, to see that you've returned. Perhaps you'd like to come with me.'

'And this time,' his short-haired companion said, 'we don't want you running off again, do we? So you'd better put these on.'

Before I knew it, he had fitted handcuffs around my wrists and I was led down the aisle of the plane in front of all those people, down the steps, into the police car, and away towards whatever fate had in store for me.

# Chapter 9  *A walk by the river*

'We're sorry to hear about your wife,' the nice policeman in the front said, as the police car crawled onto the M4 motorway for the journey into London. 'It must have been a shock.'

'Or perhaps it wasn't such a surprise,' said the one with short hair who was sitting next to me in the back. 'Perhaps you were expecting it. If you play with dangerous substances, someone always gets hurt in the end.'

'Look,' I said, feeling totally exhausted, with my wrists handcuffed, a dressing still stuck to the side of my head. 'Since we last met I've had a really terrible time, OK? I don't know anything about how my wife got to be like she was ...'

'What, dead you mean?' the man sitting next to me said nastily.

'Sergeant, please,' said the man in the front, 'that was not very nice.'

'Sorry, guv,' he said, sounding remarkably un-sorry.

'Yes,' I said evenly. I didn't even have enough energy to protest against this unfeeling cruelty. 'I have no idea how she ended up dead. I know that she was poisoned with some chemical agent, but I don't know what or how. It was nothing to do with me. My God,' I said to them, my voice rising slightly as I realised that I had nothing left to lose. 'Don't you think I would have stopped it happening if I could have done, if I'd known anything about it?'

'Well, as to that Mr Armstrong,' my companion sneered, 'how can we be sure? I mean you sound convincing, but then you would, wouldn't you, whether you knew about this or not? How do we know you're telling us the truth?'

'You know what,' I said, realising suddenly that I meant it, 'I couldn't care less if you believe me or not. There's nothing you can do to me that's worse than what's happened over the last two weeks. So if you want to imprison me, question me, beat me up, make up evidence against me, any of the things I've heard that policemen do, well go on! Go ahead. I am in your hands and there's absolutely nothing I can do about it.'

They stopped talking after that and I suppose I must have slept because the next thing I knew we had stopped at the back of a police station in central London.

'Wake up, Mr Armstrong,' said the nicer of the two, 'wake up.' I opened my eyes. They felt as if they were attached to lead weights. I wanted to go back to sleep.

'Come on, Derek,' my short-haired tormentor said, surprising me with his use of my first name. 'Time to get out and answer a few questions, don't you think?'

I climbed out of the car and they led me through a back door, down a long corridor, into a room where an older policeman sat behind a desk with a large book.

'Turn out your pockets please, sir,' he said.

'What?' I asked sleepily. 'What for?'

'Oh, come on,' said my companion. 'You must have seen films about the police, surely. We're bringing you in for questioning, aren't we? So this is the bit where we take all your possessions, anything you might have on your person which you could use to harm yourself, and the custody sergeant here, he writes it all in his big book. That way you can't come back and say we stole your wallet or anything like that. Got it?'

I got it. They took my wallet, my passport, my watch, the belt from my trousers, my credit card, an old comb, a packet of peanuts I'd pocketed from the plane, a photograph of Malgosia, a little notebook I carried around with me with notes of things I had to do, my electronic organiser and a cassette tape of Mozart's 'Symphonia Concertante' for violin and viola played by two friends of mine which I'd forgotten I had with me when I left England. Then they took me to a cell, pushed me in and shut the door.

It smelt pretty bad in there but I was pleased the room was empty. I sat on the hard, concrete bench facing the door and wondered how long I was going to stay. I wondered if they could tell me why my wife had died. I wondered who I could call to get me out of the situation I was in and then I wondered why I should care.

Once or twice over the next four hours the little metal window in the door would open and I'd see a policeman looking in at me. One of them even asked, 'You all right, mate? Can I get you a cup of tea from the machine?' and I was so amazed at this gesture of normality that I agreed. When it came the liquid was hot and sweet, and after the dryness of the aeroplane cabin, and the dryness of my soul, it was curiously refreshing.

Finally, just as I was drifting off to sleep again, the door opened and my nice policeman came in.

'How are you, Mr Armstrong?' he said. 'I see they've been looking after you.' I smiled weakly at him. The situation was so absurd and his words were so inappropriate for the mess I was in, that I couldn't help it.

'Well,' said the policeman, 'I'm glad to see that you're in a better mood. It'll make my job much easier. Would you like to come with me?'

I walked out of the cell. The short-haired policeman was standing in the corridor. The two of them walked me past the custody sergeant's desk, up a flight of stairs and into an airless little room with a table, five chairs, a fluorescent light above us and a tape recorder. We sat down, me on one side of the table, the two policemen on the other.

The short-haired policeman switched on the tape recorder and said who we were and what the time was. Then he looked at me.

'You are allowed to make one phone call, you know,' he said. 'Do you want to make a phone call?' I was going to say no, but then I suddenly thought of someone I would like to come and help me.

'Yes, please,' I said, so we all got up again, marched out of the room and into the corridor to where a payphone was fastened to the wall. I stopped.

'Well?' said the nicer of the two. 'Go on. Make your call.'

'That's a bit of a problem,' I told him. 'I had to give that sergeant all my money, didn't I? Can you lend me 20p?'

They both complained a bit at that, but eventually the younger policeman put his hand into his pocket and gave me the coin. I dialled a number and for what seemed like an age nobody answered. But they did in the end and in the background I could hear a recording of a Beethoven quartet. 'Hello,' said the voice, 'hello, can I help you?'

'Rachel,' I said, the relief in my voice making me sound almost happy. 'Rachel, I'm back in London and I need your help.'

*   *   *

Rachel sent her mother. I had forgotten that her parents were both lawyers. I had met Rachel's mother once or twice before when she had come to listen to the quartet. I remembered her as being warm and pleasant, an older version of her daughter but somehow stronger and more sure of herself. She had always been very nice to me.

In the cell with the police she wasn't particularly warm or pleasant at all, but she was strong and assertive. My nice and nasty questioners found her almost impossible to handle. Every time they asked me a question that she didn't like, she would forbid me to answer, or she would lecture the two policemen on the rules for police interrogations, rules which she knew in a great deal more detail than them. And she did it with such a severe face, such a hard determination, that my two tormentors, who had no doubt come across many lawyers before, but who had obviously not met anyone like Rachel's mother, were finally reduced to almost complete silence and, by the time we had finished, had ended up telling us far more than they had intended.

The interview started when the nice policeman asked me what I knew about Seratraxel.

'Seratraxel?' I repeated. 'What's that?'

'A chemical agent,' the short-haired one said, 'a kind of

nerve gas, I suppose you'd call it. Odourless. No smell. Takes about four or five days . . .'

'That's enough,' the older policeman said. 'Well, Mr Armstrong?'

'I don't know anything about Sera – whatever-it-is,' I replied.

'Come on,' the short-haired one continued, 'you don't expect us to believe that, do you?'

'My client has said that he doesn't know what it is,' Rachel's mother said, 'so you will have to take his word for it. You are not allowed to go on asking a witness the same question again and again.' That was the way she talked.

They tried a few more times, though, asking all sorts of clever questions. Each time Rachel's mother stepped in to protect me, though since I knew very little anyway, they would never have got much out of me.

Next they started asking me about Scotland. Had I ever been to Dundonnell?

'Dundonnell?' I answered. 'I've never heard of it.'

'Well, it appears that your wife knew where it was,' the older man said.

'She might have, but I don't. Where is it?' I asked them.

'Right up in the north of Scotland on the shores of Little Loch Broom, just south of Ullapool,' the nicer policeman said. 'It's a lovely place, a lonely place. I expect your wife told you about it, about the hotel there, the one she stayed at more than once. The only one there is in Dundonnell. She probably told you about the research station just up the mountain there. She did tell you all about that, didn't she?'

'No. No, I've never heard any of this before,' I told him truthfully. But the pieces were suddenly all beginning to fit.

'Look, Derek,' the short-haired policeman said nastily, 'all this "I don't know" doesn't impress me you know. I wasn't born yesterday. I suggest that you knew your wife went up to Dundonnell to meet a man called Tibor Arkadi, a man we can't get at because he's in Brazil where you've just been. I suggest that you knew that around the time your wife and her "companion" were up there the last time, some Seratraxel was stolen from the government chemical weapons research station, and what's more that you know where that chemical agent is now. Because we've searched your house from top to bottom, you see, but we can't find it. And let me warn you, Derek Armstrong, if you don't tell us where it is pretty damn soon, we're going to shut you away for a very, very long time. So what's it going to be? The truth? Or the rest of your life in jail?'

'Chemical agents?' Rachel's mother said unexpectedly. 'At a government research station? I thought this country had signed a convention to ban chemical weapons research.'

'Fool,' the older policeman snapped at his colleague. 'You talk a little bit too much.'

'It's not what you think,' he said to us. 'Just some research the armed forces are doing to find out what our enemies are up to. That's all. If you say anything about it no-one will believe you. Anyway, we'd lock you up straight away. So you won't want to talk about it, will you?'

They asked me more questions, and I told them what I knew (when Rachel's mother would let me). But it wasn't much. And in return they told me that they had been sent reports of a man answering Tibor Arkadi's description meeting a worker from the secret research station.

'The worker died in a car accident,' the older policeman said, 'but we think he took the Seratraxel and gave it to Mr Arkadi.'

'A most convenient accident,' the short-haired one said. But by then I'd heard enough, and once Rachel's mother had stopped the policemen asking any more questions we left the police station.

'Where to now?' she asked, but I hadn't the slightest idea what to do next. I didn't have any idea about anything really. So when she said that Rachel had offered to put me up at her house if I didn't want to go back to my own place I agreed with the suggestion because I couldn't think of any reason not to.

\* \* \*

'Come on,' Rachel said to me, 'it's a beautiful day. I think you need some fresh air.'

I looked at her. She was worried about me, I could tell. I suppose that wasn't very surprising, really. I had been staying in her house for over two weeks, and in that time, I admit it, I was terrible company. I slept a lot. I went for walks by the river (and made Rachel very nervous, she told me later, because she was afraid that I would throw myself off a bridge or something). I hardly said a word. And in all that time Rachel, my friend, my companion, never complained.

My bandage was off, and I had stopped taking the tranquillisers her doctor had given to me. Rachel had been to my house to get my viola and bring me my post (which I hadn't been interested enough to look at yet) and a couple of changes of clothes. Now she had decided that I needed organising, so she'd rung Matt and Carl, asked them round, and with her sister (who's an excellent pianist) we had just played through the quintet by Elgar. And while we were playing I had only thought of Malgosia and policemen and men with guns firing up at me about three or four times instead of every minute as I had been doing recently.

That's the thing about music, of course: it demands all your attention, all your concentration. Once we were in the middle of the first movement, I had my first moment of real peace since Malgosia had left – if peace is surrendering yourself to the demands of music-making as I was doing. Admittedly I wasn't playing my best, but I got through it, and though Matt and Carl looked vaguely disapproving, Rachel smiled over at me after each movement, a smile of real encouragement, real hope.

We stood up, leaving our instruments on the chairs. Matt invited Rachel's sister for an early evening drink and Carl said he had to phone his parents. Rachel took me by the arm and walked to the door.

Outside it was warmer than I had expected. The sky was a bright autumn blue and there wasn't a cloud in the sky. We turned right and walked down to the path that runs alongside the River Thames. Other people were out too; an elderly couple walking their dog, a sweaty jogger pounding past us with the *ticka-ticka-ticka* of her walkman echoing tunelessly as she brushed my shoulder on her energetic journey.

'Look,' said Rachel as we were passing a pub that seemed vaguely familiar. 'Remember that place?' She was smiling broadly, the evening light glittering in her pretty eyes. I remembered the place all right from that night back when we were both students, and for a second, even after all these years, I felt embarrassed.

'Disaster Inn!' she said, and laughed and there was something so innocent about it that I laughed back at her. I felt incredibly grateful that she could joke about it now. It was a subject we had not mentioned for a long time.

'Dee!' she cried. 'You laughed. You actually laughed. I can't believe it. That must be the first time for days.'

'Yes, well, there hasn't been much to laugh about.' I said. 'But look, I'm sorry, really sorry I've been so terrible. You've been so kind. I don't know how I'll ever be able to thank you.'

'Poor Dee,' she said, holding my arm tighter, 'what are we going to do with you?'

'I don't know,' I replied, watching two boats with eight rowers each racing under Putney bridge, the cries of the coxes in the back of each boat ringing across the water like ghosts. 'It's just that I can't stop it, you see. I can't get that picture out of my head, the man in his white protection suit carrying Malgosia to that plane, and the hospital, and that bastard Tibor and . . .'

'Derek,' Rachel said, using my full name for once, turning me round and making me face her, 'Derek, I know you must be hurting, we all know that, and I'm not trying to say it's not important or anything, please believe me, but now it's time to stop it. It's over. The past has passed. It's the future we should be thinking of. It's the future that matters to you. To me.'

And before I could stop her she had kissed me, and suddenly, as if I had always known this, I felt an overpowering sense of love for her and a great tide of relief washing over me. I don't know how you sense these things, but then and there, as the evening light cast its gentle shadows over the river's edge, I knew with absolute certainty that I could trust this woman, that I had always been able to trust this woman with my life.

'Rachel,' I whispered, 'help me.'

'You silly fool,' she said, tears in her pretty eyes. 'Of course I'll help you. I've always helped you. Help you do what?'

I told her and she started to protest, but she must have seen my determination so in the end she stopped talking and we held each other as the tide came in and the water rippled over the mud. Then we turned and walked back to the house. I kept looking at her as if she was someone I had never met before, someone I had never really seen before. For the first time since the day when I had come home to find my wife gone, I felt as if something positive might happen. But there was danger too. Back in Rio where I had suddenly realised that I had to return.

# Chapter 10   *Sugar Loaf Mountain*

For a moment I thought I wasn't going to be able to make it. The sweat was pouring down my face, and my fingers were slipping all over the place. The others weren't much better either. Rachel's left hand was sliding on strings that were threatening to go out of tune because of the heat. I saw her frown as she played, fighting the heat. But then, suddenly, we were there; the fast presto at the very end of Schubert's 'Death and the Maiden' quartet, and however hot and bothered I felt I just had to keep playing to keep up with the others, faster and faster as the movement rushed towards its climax and, amazingly, we played the final chord with a burst of energy that none of us were really feeling.

In the front row of the audience I saw Paul dig Oswaldo in the side to wake him up. The Cuban detective's head went back and his eyes opened wide with fright until, realising where he was, he started clapping along with everyone else.

'Bravo!' the beautiful Sandra cried, wildly enthusiastic, and her call was taken up by the rest of the Brazilian audience so that we received almost a standing ovation from the five hundred people in the hall.

'All right, all right,' Carl whispered across to me as we stood to take our bows, 'I admit it. You were right.' He was talking about the long discussions we had had, with me trying to persuade him to come to Brazil for a concert tour and him saying it wasn't worth it, no-one would appreciate us there. But I went on. It would be a wonderful opportunity, I told him, we could really make a name for ourselves in Latin America, it would be a good way of starting again. I knew I had nearly destroyed the quartet, I told him, and this was my way of trying to make it up to all of them.

In the end I persuaded him and Matt. Even Rachel agreed, but it was more difficult for her because she knew that my motives weren't just musical, and she knew that what I was thinking of could be very dangerous. I think we were both nervous, actually. Having just discovered each other properly for the first time, the last thing either of us needed was to lose the other. Rachel's love was bringing me back to life. I could feel the pieces of myself putting themselves back together like a multi-dimensional puzzle, all the bits falling into place, all the failures and sadnesses falling away from me. I noticed that now when the sun shone, I heard the music of the birds and the lap of water. My past with Malgosia and the terrible thing that had happened to her was shared knowledge between us, something Rachel and I could talk about openly.

She knew that the one thing I could not yet do was lose the hatred I felt for Tibor, my rival. Of course we had both discussed the possibility that my anger was really directed at Malgosia or myself for all those years when I had tried to love someone who never felt the same about me. It is certainly true that when I looked back at my marriage I felt this cold sense of failure. But there was something else that was far stronger: a conviction that people like Tibor should not be allowed to play with other people's lives.

When the decision to come to Brazil had been taken, our agent started working right away, contacting the Brazilian embassy, the British Council, anyone she could think of, and pretty soon we had a tour planned taking us from Recife to Porto Alegre, from São Paulo to Salvador. And of course, at the end of a very successful series of concerts, here we were in Rio for our last performance. Paul had helped with the organisation and tonight's concert was the result of all his efforts.

We had a party after the show. People came up to us and congratulated us. Paul was really pleased with the result of his efforts, and Sandra, who had loved the music, was obviously fascinated by Carl. Matt seemed to be having a good time too, surrounded by a group of admiring men and women. As for me I found myself standing on my own for a moment while Rachel went to get us another drink.

'He's agreed,' Oswaldo said quietly, coming up to me, pushing out clouds of smoke from his enormous cigar. 'He'll meet you.'

Not for the first time I suddenly felt almost uncontrollable fear. I wished I hadn't started this. For the thousandth time I wished I had never heard of Tibor Arkadi.

'He'll be on Sugar Loaf Mountain tomorrow at two o'clock,' Oswaldo went on, making sure that no-one else could hear us. 'He'll meet you in the restaurant. He says he won't talk to you unless you come on your own.'

'How do I know that he won't have a whole army of his "friends" with him?' I asked.

'You don't. But you're the one asking for this meeting, remember, not him, so you have to do what he says.'

'Great!' I replied. Suddenly all my plans, everything I was going to say, sounded stupid.

Rachel returned with two glasses. She looked from Oswaldo to me and then back again.

'Tibor's going to meet him?' she asked the detective. Oswaldo glanced at me and I nodded.

'Yes,' he told her, 'tomorrow.'

'Oh God,' Rachel said, suddenly gripping my arm. 'Please be careful. I've only just found you. I couldn't bear to lose you so soon.'

\* \* \*

When I got out of the cable car the sun hit me right between the eyes. I took my sunglasses out of my pocket and put them on. I walked towards the restaurant on legs that seemed to be moving by themselves. It was like doing a really frightening musical audition where you walk into a room and it's all silent and three people are there waiting for you to play, ready to judge you, and you're so scared that you seem to do everything automatically, all the time wishing you could be somewhere else, your heart beating loudly in your ears, sure that you are going to fail, but knowing that now there was no turning back. That's how it was as I walked towards my meeting with Tibor. Except that it was worse.

I thought about Rachel back at the hotel, about Oswaldo who I knew would be coming up Sugar Loaf Mountain any minute now, even though I had told him not to. They couldn't help me, though, either of them.

Tibor was sitting against one of the large windows in the restaurant so that his head was almost in silhouette and his face was in shadow. He was wearing dark glasses himself, and when I came up to him his expression did not change.

'Mr Derek Armstrong,' he said icily. 'How nice to see you again after all these years. You still play the viola, I am told.'

'Yes,' I replied, furious because just when I really didn't want it to happen, my voice was shaking, 'but you abandoned music, I am told.'

'Boring,' was his reply, 'playing the same old dead composers' music again and again.'

'You'd know a lot about death, I suppose,' I told him.

'Ah,' Tibor said, 'Malgosia. Yes, well you certainly don't waste time in small talk, do you? I didn't mean for her to die, you know. That wasn't part of the plan.'

'What plan?' I asked, feeling suddenly angry. 'What plan? Wasn't playing with her emotions enough for you? Wasn't causing chaos in her family enough for you? Wasn't ruining Anja's life amusing enough? You had to destroy Malgosia too? My God, what is it that makes you do all these things?'

'Well, well!' Tibor replied nastily. 'The little viola player is making brave speeches, isn't he? Maybe you have got a backbone after all, despite what she said.'

That hurt. That really hurt. But I had to keep calm if I wanted to learn the truth, if I wanted to survive this meeting. Otherwise I'd jump over the table and try to kill him and that would probably be the end of me.

'Go on then,' I said, trying to sound as normal as possible. 'Tell me. How did Malgosia get poisoned? Why did you go back to her after all those years?'

'And if I tell you, what then? What's in it for me?' said my wife's lover, turning away from me in a calculated gesture of scorn. 'Your messenger, that ridiculous Cuban, said you had something for me, something I would want. That's why I agreed to meet you here.'

'Oh, I've got something for you,' I replied, taking a small packet from my pocket. 'It's this.'

'Well?' he said, puzzled now by what I was doing. 'What is it?'

'Just a little chemical compound,' I replied, looking straight at him, and taking a small glass container from the packet. 'It's called Seratraxel, I believe. I found it in Malgosia's jewellery box. Just before we left England. With a note telling me what it was. I think she must have put it there as a kind of insurance policy, in case you tried to mess around with her. Except that it didn't work for her, did it, and I want to know why not.'

Tibor was staring hard at the glass container in my hand. 'I don't believe you. You're bluffing,' he said, a slight smile playing on his face. 'She gave me all the Seratraxel she brought over here.'

'I'm afraid you're wrong there,' I told him. 'She kept some of it back.' I could see the uncertainty, the fear on his face. 'Now, here's the plan,' I went on. 'I'm going to unscrew the stopper from this little glass tube ...' I held it up in front of him. 'And then I'm going to give it to you. I reckon you'll live for about five or six days after that.'

Tibor looked at me. He believed me now. He stood up. He was going to try and get past me. I saw him signal to someone behind me. But I had been ready for this. I stood up too, right in front of him and held out the glass phial, as if to drop it.

'You wouldn't dare!' he whispered. His face had gone white. For the first time he looked less sure of himself. 'It would kill you too.'

'Well, of course it would, you fool,' I told him. I enjoyed saying that. 'But then I don't have anything left to live for, do I? You took my wife away from me, so I might as well get something out of finishing my miserable life by ending yours.'

'Wh-wh-what about the other people in the restaurant?' he stammered, drops of sweat beginning to appear on his forehead, running down his temples.

'Tough. Just their bad luck. Wrong place, wrong time. We've all got to die sometime after all. Now why don't we sit down again and go on with our conversation?' I had him in my power. He sat down heavily. He wiped his face with a napkin from the table in front of him.

'What do you want?' he said, trying to re-establish some authority.

'The truth,' I told him, 'just the truth. For example, why did you do it? Why did you get in touch with Malgosia again? Why did you involve her in your horrible little crimes? Why on earth did she have to die?'

'And if I tell you, you'll stop messing about with that nerve gas?'

'Oh yes. In fact you can have it. I'm sure the extra will come in useful,' I said.

'All right,' he agreed, 'all right. What do you want to know?'

'How did my wife die?'

'It was her decision,' Tibor said. 'A stupid decision. She nearly killed us all.'

'What on earth are you talking about?'

'Women are strange, don't you find?' he asked. I could see him thinking of what to say to me. I held out the glass phial again.

'All right! All right!' he said. 'Look, Malgosia agreed to bring the Seratraxel over here. We put it in the three valves of a trumpet and she brought the trumpet over here. I didn't realise that she'd kept some for herself.' He looked over to the other side of the restaurant where two men, his bodyguards, I imagine, were watching us as we spoke. I had to go on quickly.

'Why did she agree to help you?' I asked him. 'Wasn't it dangerous?'

'She loved me,' he said simply.

'What exactly were you doing, Tibor?' I asked, amazed at his sudden self-control. 'What were you up to? Why would you want this deadly chemical anyway?'

'That is something you do not have to know. All I can say is that some people – you don't need to know from where – needed the formula for this particular chemical agent and they were prepared to pay a great deal of money to get samples for them to analyse. I haven't the slightest idea what they are going to do with it. That's not my concern.'

'Of course it's your concern. You can't just wash your hands of something like this. It's criminal!' My voice was getting louder. People were looking at us.

Tibor laughed. 'Oh dear, is the little viola player worried because it's a bit criminal? Of course it's criminal! Everything I do is "criminal" in your terms, in your boring little life, and you know what? I like "criminal", I like my life, I like the money, the power, the danger. These are things you will never understand.'

'So how did she get sick?' I asked him, ignoring his speech.

'She opened up one of the containers. She did it on purpose. She knew what she was doing.' He was looking uncomfortable.

'You're telling me that Malgosia exposed herself to this stuff on purpose? But why? What could have made her do such a thing?'

'Look,' Tibor said, gesturing with his arms. He was suddenly desperate. 'Look, I liked Malgosia, all right? I've always liked her. I liked her sister too. It was fun to see them go crazy over me, you know. I liked that especially. And it was good to have someone like Anja waiting for me when I was over in Central Europe. It passed the time on my visits there. But I got bored with her in the end. So I got in touch with Malgosia again. For fun. Come on, don't look at me like that. You're a man. You know the score. We're all the same underneath. Anyway,' he continued quickly seeing the anger in my face, 'Malgosia was so grateful. I couldn't believe it. After all that time. And then I suddenly realised she could help me with my little problem of how to get the nerve gas from Scotland to Brazil. No-one would suspect a musician, after all. No-one is going to search a trumpet case. So we gave her the trumpet and I came back here. I told her to wait until I contacted her.' He stopped. He folded his arms.

'Tibor,' I said to him, 'you haven't finished.'

'No,' he agreed unwillingly. 'No. I misjudged it, you see.

I was negotiating with my clients, trying to get them to pay more, keeping them waiting. Only I got it wrong and they got really angry. You know – "if we don't get the Seratraxel sample in the next few days you will be in trouble" – that kind of thing. I believed them. So I had to e-mail her and ring her. Get her to come here immediately. Good old Malgosia. She came straight away!'

'You still haven't finished,' I said when his voice died away for the second time.

'Look,' he started again, 'she knew what I was like. I never promised her anything. Honestly. From the very beginning, all those years ago, she knew what I was like. But she must have thought that because she'd done this thing for me, that I would be grateful or something. She asked me to marry her, you see. She'd get a divorce, she said. We could live together for ever. Here in Brazil. Anywhere. She said she'd always wanted that.'

His words were coming out at great speed now, as if he wanted to get the story over with quickly, as if he was, unbelievably, ashamed of himself.

'And I told her not to be so stupid. I told her she was living in a land of make-believe. The idea of it! Me? Tibor, settling down with one woman. I laughed at her and, well I shouldn't have done it, I suppose, but how was I to know what she would do?'

'What did she do?' I yelled at him, though I knew of course.

'She opened up one of the containers,' he sighed, looking away from me. 'I only just had time to run out of the room. I slammed the door. Got the people to come down from Rio with their chemical suits, all their chemical equipment. They cleaned the place up in no time. It was too late for your wife, of course. But you know that. I mean, I knew she liked me, but honestly, Derek,' he said using my first name as if, suddenly, we were friends, 'to kill yourself for love! That's just ridiculous. She must have been mad or something.'

So that was it. I had my story. And suddenly the fury which I had managed to keep bottled up inside me exploded. I started to unscrew the stopper from the little glass tube.

'What are you doing?' Tibor cried, aghast. 'What do you think you're doing?'

'If it was good enough for Malgosia, it's good enough for you,' I said with a forced laugh.

'Stop it! Stop it!' the man in front of me yelled, standing up. 'You don't know what you're doing!'

'Oh, but I do,' I replied, 'I know exactly what I'm doing.' And I took off the stopper.

That's when Tibor lost it completely. He leapt on to the table and jumped over me. He fell badly on the floor but he picked himself up and half ran out of the restaurant. I followed him, holding the glass phial out in front of me like some religious offering. I could sense his bodyguards running behind me. Tibor kept looking back at me as he tried to run faster on his injured ankle.

He climbed the steps to the cable car station. People were just getting into one of the cars for the journey back down to ground level. Tibor pushed past them, knocking one old lady to the ground.

'Watch out!' he cried in Portuguese. 'He's got poison!' And when people didn't move out of his way, he changed it.

'He's got a bomb!' he shouted, 'he's got a bomb.'

People ran away then. Tibor rushed into the car and tried to close the door, pulling desperately on the control handle to start his descent. I reached the concrete platform a few seconds later. The car started its journey. I wrenched open the door and jumped in just as we moved away from the platform and the mountainside dropped vertically away from us.

'Keep away from me!' Tibor screamed as we gathered speed. 'Keep away from me!'

'Or what?' I shouted back at him, 'or you'll kill me? It's a bit late for that, isn't it?' I moved closer towards him.

He jumped past me and ran back to the door, wrenching it open in his turn. An alarm bell started ringing. Tibor edged out of the car and started climbing its side. Now we were rocking backwards and forwards violently as we travelled downwards. I followed Malgosia's lover out into space.

When I think of it now I go cold with fear. I cannot believe that I ended up on the roof of a cable car with nothing between me and the ground except hundreds of feet of empty space. But then I was working on auto-pilot, hardly conscious of where I was, quite able to climb up the side of the swaying cable car out there in space. I'd have climbed Mount Everest if you had asked me. And when I got onto the roof, close to the wheels as they turned over and over on the thick steel cable, I found Tibor crouching there, shivering with fear, the strong man made weak, the unfeeling lover suddenly feeling real emotion for the first time, probably, in his horrible life. He looked pathetic.

'Here,' I said, holding up the glass phial. 'You can have this. It isn't Seratraxel anyway. It's Malgosia's favourite perfume, that's all. Just my little joke. To remind you of her.' And I threw it at him.

Poor old Tibor. He obviously didn't hear me. He didn't understand me anyway. He jumped up in horror, lost his balance, and for a terrible moment he tried desperately to keep his footing on the edge of the car. His arms waved around in panic. Half sounds, half words came from his terrified mouth. He knew he was going to fall. And then he was gone and I was left empty-handed as the wires sang and the oiled wheels turned over and over in the warm afternoon air.

# Chapter 11  *Romantic love*

It wasn't a fancy wedding. No white dresses or churches or anything like that. It didn't seem appropriate somehow. But it was still one of the happiest days of my life, my second marriage, and for once the sun shone and I knew I was never going to regret this day.

Rachel looked absolutely beautiful. She'd made herself a red and blue dress that was just right for her beautiful figure and seemed to pick out the light in her warm brown eyes. I had bought a new suit, and the registry office, which was crowded with friends and family, was full of sunshine for the brief ceremony.

Afterwards we went back to her mother's house and had one of the best parties I have ever been to. Carl and Matt played violin duets and then a friend of Matt's set up with his band and we danced to old hit tunes. Even my parents got up and danced at one stage, and looking at them, I realised how pleased I was that we had re-established contact again, now that I was with a woman they really liked.

It was strange this feeling of happiness. It didn't seem right somehow. I wasn't used to it. But as Rosemary had told us a week ago, 'you can't live in the past forever. The things that happened to you weren't your <u>fault</u>. You aren't responsible for Tibor,' she told me, 'and I know that you blame yourself for what happened to Malgosia, but she made her own decisions, not you.'

'That's what I've been trying to tell him,' Rachel agreed with her. They had become good friends, my soon-to-be-second wife and my first wife's best friend. They had got to know each other when we came back from Brazil and I had felt I had to let Rosemary in on everything that had happened. So I told her about Seratraxel and disappointed love, about the hole where Tibor's heart should have been, and about how when Tibor had disappeared off the cable car roof, I had suddenly realised that I too might fall. I knew I wasn't brave enough to climb down the side of the cabin again. But then I realised, with relief, that there was a skylight in the roof and I managed to break it and fall into the interior of the car where I lay shivering with fear and misery until the cabin came to a stop. I got out with shaking legs to see Rachel and Paul and a bunch of policemen waiting to talk to me.

It was Oswaldo who saved the situation. He had reached the top of Sugar Loaf Mountain just as Tibor had run from the restaurant with me in hot pursuit. He managed to persuade the police that Tibor had gone crazy and that I had tried to save him. Pretty soon, instead of treating me like a murderer, they started to think of me as a hero and for a day I was the darling of the press. Without getting any information from me (because I did not trust myself to say anything) the reporters built up a whole story about a courageous Englishman, a musician, who had tried desperately to save the life of a stranger.

And then we left Brazil and flew back to England. I knew I had to get home before more people started asking more questions. And this time when I got home, with help from Rachel's mother, I went back to see my two policemen friends and told them everything that Tibor had told me. For all I know secret services all over the world are still hunting down Tibor's clients and contacts – at least I hope they are. And that was pretty much the end of that except for the nightmares when I wake from some fresh terror to hear Rachel's gentle voice in my ear telling me that everything is all right.

And it is all right. I keep telling myself it is all right. But there's this dark pain in my heart which I am trying hard to move but which I fear may never go away. I have experienced things I had never looked for and I even ended up killing a man – or at the very least contributing towards his death. And however much I tell myself that he deserved it, still I can't help believing that I did something terribly wrong. So when Rachel tells me I am good I tell her I believe her and she is content, and maybe, just maybe in time she will convince me that she is right.

When our wedding band had a break for a drink the four of us, our quartet, played a cheerful piece by Haydn, 'The Lark' and then we gave our audience some of Matt's arrangements of popular songs and everyone clapped. It was Rachel's idea that we should play, not just because that's what we did together, but also to celebrate the fact that we'd just got our first recording contract and that, after our honeymoon, we were starting on a tour of the British Isles. Things were looking good, I told myself as we packed up our instruments when the band started again, and if I could just stop thinking of Malgosia they would get better and better.

Later, as it began to get dark, and the music had turned from fast and furious, to slow and peaceful, Rachel and I found ourselves talking to Rosemary, Matt and Carl – and Sandra, who had flown over from Rio for the wedding, though I suspect her visit was more to do with seeing Carl again than it was to see me getting married!

'Are you really all right now?' Matt said. 'After all the things that happened to you.'

'Come on, Matt,' Rosemary said. (She'd only met him that afternoon, but Matt's like that. They were already good friends.) 'Now is hardly the time.'

'It's all right, Rosemary,' I told her before turning to the others. 'Don't worry, Matt, I've never been righter you know. I should have done this years ago, got together with Rachel, properly I mean, and if I had – well, think of all the things that might not have happened.'

'It's not your fault, sweetheart,' Rachel said, 'you know it's not your fault.' She kissed me and the others clapped.

'Romantic love,' Matt laughed. 'Doesn't it make you sick!'

'Are you jealous?' said Rosemary.

'Of course not,' Matt replied, and then he blushed. 'Well, maybe just a little.'

'Well, don't be,' Rosemary said. 'Happiness doesn't come very often you know, and all of us, me and you Matt, Sandra there and Carl, maybe we're all going to be happy one day. Maybe not. But meanwhile let's just celebrate these two lovely people, on this fabulous day!' Then she sat down rather heavily. I think she had drunk a bit too much champagne.

'No-one would believe your story if you wrote it down,' Carl said suddenly. 'It's too fantastic, too extraordinary.'

'Yes, why don't you write it down?' Matt asked, looking hopefully at Rosemary for support, but getting no reply.

'No,' Rachel said. 'They'd think he'd made it all up.'

'So he can write it as a novel,' Matt replied and everybody laughed.

'I don't think so,' I said, 'I want to live in the present and the future, not the past. It's what's going to happen next that matters.' I put my arm round my new wife's shoulders. 'What happened back then, all that is over. Finished. I've left it all behind.'

But of course I lied. The past is always with us.